ACADEMIC PROCESSION

ACADEMIC PROCESSION

Reflections of a College President

By HENRY M. WRISTON

Columbia University Press
NEW YORK 1959

Library of Congress Catalog Card Number: 59-10476

Published in Great Britain, Canada, India, and Pakistan
by the Oxford University Press
London, Toronto, Bombay, and Karachi

Manufactured in the United States of America

In Memory of

R. B. W.

Foreword

THIS is an intensely personal book, consisting of reflections upon experiences of more than thirty years. There is critical comment about persons, but what is written is wholly without malice. I have limited myself to episodes which influenced my course or my views of the presidency.

This book was suggested by my wife and would never have been finished but for her continuous encouragement. As in all previous books, I must acknowledge the help of Ruth E. Sandborn—her precise memory, her critical eye and unfaltering assistance. Mrs. Dorothea Borden has been associated with Miss Sandborn and has prepared the copy with skill and unfailing good nature.

HENRY M. WRISTON

New York, N.Y.
February 6, 1959

Contents

I

Background for a Presidency

I BECAME a college president—in my mind—during my junior year in college. Disillusioned, I abandoned the office—in the same way—at the age of thirty-two. On my thirty-sixth birthday I again changed my mind and entered upon a lifetime career.

Each decision was made under dramatic circumstances. They were such exciting episodes that they remain engraved upon my memory far too deeply to be erased. Moreover, they gave me, long before I actually took office, both the bright and the dark sides of the adventure. When I entered upon the substance of the task, therefore, it was with few illusions. Instead, there was a profound commitment, one which was not to be shaken by the great depression, with its tragic academic consequences, or the Second World War, with its even more desperate influences upon education.

The glamor belonged to that first awakening of ambition. It was associated with the formal inauguration of a new president for Wesleyan University in which, by a series of coincidences, I became an active participant.

Academic excellence had no part in that first experience. I went to college as naturally and as inevitably as though no other course of action were possible. My father had broken away from surroundings that supplied no stimulus to education—or indeed to ambition. To earn money for his own education, he taught school before he finished his preparatory work. He paid his way at every step. After preparatory study at Ohio Wesleyan—and more teaching—he set out for the new University of Denver and worked his way through by preaching in nearby communities. Then, with a wife and two children, he left Wyoming for Boston and theological school. He remained a scholar and teacher during his successive pastorates; education meant so much to him that when he could not earn enough to cover its cost he borrowed. He was not out of debt for his long schooling until I was in college.

My mother had been a Colorado school teacher. After marriage she studied all the courses father took, at the same time performing her domestic duties and fulfilling the multifold church obligations which fall upon the preacher's unpaid colleague.

Both took college for granted for their sons—and so did the sons. This had a profound effect which few people would now suspect. I went to college for no purpose except the experience itself; it seemed to me then—and has ever since—an adequate objective. There was, naturally, a dim awareness that someday I should have to make up my mind regarding a career. But I entered college in 1907 with no vocational objective and no deep concern about one. It was all new and I wanted all of it. No college experience passed me by. I learned to dance and missed only one dance in my four years. Six feet tall and weighing 128 pounds, I played scrub basketball. I worked on, and finally edited, the college paper. At first normal industry and the admonitions of my brother, three years ahead of me, made me do respectable but undistinguished scholastic work.

Before college days I had become accustomed to earning

some part—indeed a growing part—of my own expenses. Once I listed twenty different ways in which I had earned money before going to college. Doubtless some of them involved "exploitation" which present child labor laws would prohibit. As a bellhop in a country hotel during a summer vacation at the end of my sophomore year in high school, my working schedule averaged fourteen hours a day, seven days a week. The salary was ten dollars a month; tips (including earnings from a shoeshine chair) amounted to about a dollar and a half a day. And the word "hop" in my title was no euphemism; on one occasion I climbed twenty-eight flights of stairs, by count, before nine in the morning. What people did with all that ice water I have never known.

It was my initiation into a full-time job, and an eye opener. I learned at first hand the tyranny of a chef: his worst threat was to feed us nothing but tripe—and I have never been able to face it since. I knew the misery of being fired, for no reason and by an absentee proprietor, when I had no place to go and no money to get there. In a hotel which was not careful of its clientele, except to exclude Jews even when its rooms were half empty, one saw all sorts of people and was subjected to an astounding number of propositions, none designed for a boy's health or welfare. After the experiences of that summer, I was never again tempted to take virtue for granted or to expect everything to be all for the best in a sunny world.

Selling books, my next full-time summer job, proved just as revealing in a different way, and far more lucrative. The difference between the outside of a house and the inside, the motivations that caused people to buy or refuse to subscribe—these and many more observations of human nature were essential elements in my education.

The occupation which was most agreeable, easiest, and, all things considered, the most rewarding financially was writing for the newspapers at space rates—ten cents an inch. Learning that names make news and cultivating a wide acquaintance constituted the "training." The only trick was to get the assignment; that accomplished, the rest was easy. It often meant no more than rewriting something I had seen handed in for the high school or college paper.

With this background and experience I could go to college for its own sake with no anxious thought for the morrow. A scholarship, space writing, summer book selling, borrowing, and a modest allowance from home took care of finances. Vocational choice could wait. People talk of "preparation for life"; whatever meaning that inane phrase was supposed to possess, it had none for me. I was living already and having many very real experiences. How one could be more alive I could not then see—and never have since.

During my freshman year the college president seemed a very dim figure. Bearded, dignified, remote, absent from the campus most of the time, he moved in an orbit far removed from mine. There was no such thing as an "administration." The president and the superintendent of buildings had the same patronymic: one was Doctor Raymond, the other "Doc" Raymond. Of the two, "Doc" was the older, the more heavily bearded, and infinitely more ubiquitous. In our daily experience he was the more influential. There was no dean; a classics professor was "secretary of the faculty" and did the work of registrar; the librarian was a man of many duties—bursar, assistant treasurer, business manager. All shared the services of a single stenographer. There can be little wonder that the post of college president then held no appeal; I scarcely knew it existed.

During my sophomore year, however, the drama began to unfold. The trustees elected a new president, who was not to take office for several months. But, as was then customary and still is, the new man was pictured as having all the virtues. He was "young," though forty-seven did not seem young to me. He was "vigorous"; I should have used the word "nervous." He had "charm." And so on through the usual catalogue of adjectives by which a new principal figure is introduced to an academic society. Attention was centered upon him.

By merest chance I was to be brought into close contact with developments. My space-writing post with the best newspaper was given to a football player, whose stories I often wrote. I was compensated by being made publicity director for the college at a weekly salary—five dollars, if my memory is correct. In this task I was supervised by a professor of physics who had no interest, no experience, and no taste for the task. His supervision was, therefore, mild indeed and consisted of encouragement rather than correction.

The important result was that the appointment carried me into the "inside." I now shared the services of the one secretary with the president and the secretary of the faculty. A more absurd situation could hardly be imagined. Yet everyone took it in stride—except the secretary. She was extremely efficient, and just as obviously outraged. My first dictation was a letter to the *Springfield Republican.* I began boldly enough, but the sight of that poised pen and grim expression unnerved me completely; after a sentence or two I had to quit with a lame excuse. That night I composed and memorized the letter, and dictated it next day. The gambit did not fool Miss Dickson in the least, but it touched her sense of humor and we became lifelong friends. She taught me how to dictate, and what to leave to her. Thus I was early initiated into how much a good secretary can do, in many instances a lot better than her "boss." From the end of my sophomore year to this day I have never been tempted to underestimate good secretaries. They have saved me many weary hours of sheer drudgery and, from time to time, have tactfully tempered the heats of my epistolary anger.

In the fall of 1909, at the opening of my junior year, all was a-bustle in preparation for the inauguration of President Shanklin. He was full of action, and a second secretary was added. She was younger and, while very skillful, far less professional in spirit than her colleague. She was also a very pretty girl who employed all the aids to beauty permitted a half century ago. It was my first experience with glamor, and a heady one.

Far more significant than my passing infatuation was the revelation, at second hand, of the extremely human side of the man whose praises were being sung and whom I was seeking so industriously to publicize. It transpired that he dictated the letters he sent to his mother; further, they followed a well-standardized pattern of family news which lent itself to ready mockery. After transcribing one of these letters the two secretaries, under the mischievous lead of the younger, recited a kind of litany, poking fun at the clichés which they had to repeat so often and found so tiresome. Their mockery was lighthearted, but devastating. It was said long ago that "no man is a hero to his valet," and it was then borne in upon me that few men, if any, are heroes in the eyes of their secretaries.

At last the great day of the inauguration arrived. The new president had a barber come to his house at four o'clock in the morning to shave him and trim his hair. To a college boy in his whipcord "uniform" this was an awesome performance. It was obvious that he, at least, was profoundly impressed with the significance of the occasion. Then came the dignitaries: college presidents, literally by the score; the senior Senator from New York, Elihu Root, former Secretary of War and Secretary of State; the Vice President of the United States, James Schoolcraft Sherman; and, finally, President William Howard Taft, who was brought through the town to the college in triumphal procession.

No college building could hold the throng, so the opera house was rented. The academic procession fascinated me; I had a ringside seat in the theater box office. My special position let me witness a tense tussle between academic and military protocol. The new college president insisted that the place of honor in an academic procession is at the end; he proposed to march in that position with President Taft. But the President's military aide, Major Archie Butt, absolutely refused to walk in front of his commander-in-chief. So, to the disgust and fury of the new president, the place of honor went to a major. As the procession came to its end President Shanklin spied me and called out, "Good morning, Hennery"—an unfailing argot. President Taft noticed the odd pronunciation of my name and with a broad grin echoed, "Good morning, Hennery."

It was a day full of excitement for the junior who went everywhere, saw everyone, and heard everything. The inevitable conclusion was: "This is the life." I decided to accept the inevitable and make it my career.

Time dimmed the vision. The color and ceremony, the big men with big names disappeared. The new president began to do things of which the undergraduates disapproved; the pedestal, already cracked by the sardonic comments of the secretaries, was shattered.

Nevertheless, though the star did not shine so brightly, it was still there. Its partial eclipse was due in part to my realization that there was no obvious pathway toward the goal. Scholarship might seem the best road, but few of the presidents who had attended the inauguration were great scholars. Many were preachers, like the fraternal speaker from Brown, the felicitous W. H. P. Faunce. Some had been professors, like another speaker, whose academic distinction was not so marked as his family connection. The vogue for businessmen, military figures, and political names had not yet begun. Even in those early days I had some awareness—later to be sharpened immensely—of the role of chance. Our new president had no ties of any kind with the college; his choice over other men was clearly the result of a series of accidental circumstances and acquaintanceships.

However, I soon decided on the road of scholarship. The immediate effect was to alter my relationship to scholastic work. From being a casual student I became an earnest one. Without giving up any aspect of college life, I put books first and began to find the satisfactions that lie in hard intellectual labor.

Once I was set upon that path, the star became only a far-off twinkle. The scholastic grind for the rest of college and the three years in Harvard Graduate School was hard enough and long enough to absorb my full energies without dreaming of what might happen some day in the distant future.

Starting up the academic ladder was no picnic. In 1914 jobs were far from plentiful. After three years of intensive work I returned to Wesleyan with an instructorship, at $1,200. No one should be deceived into the belief that even in those days the cost of living was so low that such a salary was adequate for a newly married couple. During my first year the World War broke out, and when, three years later, I had attained a salary of $1,500, eggs were selling for a dollar a dozen and sugar for over twenty cents a pound.

The position was arduous. I was required to teach three courses, none of them in the field of specialization in which I had been trained. My graduate work was in medieval history; I had taken no courses in American history, and only one relating to government—a course in political theory by a newly appointed young lawyer. Yet I was required to teach American history, American government—municipal, state, and national—and comparative government. I had had no instruction in two of the subjects and no graduate work in the third. To "keep me busy" I was assigned for the balance of my instructional quota (five courses) to reference work in the library. It was backbreaking for a beginner.

The library assignment proved a valuable experience, for it provided first-hand knowledge of how students prepared papers; it emphasized the time and effort wasted by crude procedures. As a result my teaching techniques were altered. I came to stress written work and the best methods of preparing it. In the long run it also proved valuable for administrative purposes; when a college president has had practical experience in the daily operation of the library he has much more sympathy with the librarian's problems—fiscal, administrative, disciplinary, and instructional.

Furthermore, when I began to teach not only was the work exhausting, but the prospects for the future were not bright. Each year the president called me into his office and recited the same formula: "Hennery,"—this never changed either—"we like your work, but, as you know, we intend to have only one professor in the department, so we cannot offer you promotion here." Each year after this solemn ritual I returned home and, with the bitterness of youth, said to my wife, "The old fool doesn't see what is happening under his nose—and by his own efforts. The place is growing so fast he will *have* to appoint extra professors."

Then the war came to America, and the whole academic pattern was disrupted. Having been rejected for military service, I taught the manual of arms, "The Stakes of the War," and whatever else was required. But not for long; this time the president had a new formula: "Hennery, we like your work, but we don't see how we can pay your salary. Will you try to find some other way to earn your living until the war ends?"

I cannot remember feeling any alarm at the change in my prospects. As a boy I had turned my hand to so many kinds of work that a new shift did not seem fatal. In any event, it triggered one of those accidental chains of circumstance that are often decisive in shaping one's life. While serving as a "Four-Minute Man," speaking in theaters on the meaning of the war, and selling Liberty Bonds in a street booth, I had become interested in more efficient ways of raising money for war service agencies. Community funds in Rochester, Detroit, and other cities had included all such activities in "War Chests." Our community was plagued with a series of "drives" which were more exhaustive of energy than productive of money.

The Connecticut State Council of Defense commissioned me to write a report on War Chest practices. The idea was to make rapidly available to any Connecticut community the entire process which had been developed elsewhere. This began my tutelage in administration under one of the most extraordinary men I have ever known, the late Joseph Alsop, father of the well-known news commentators Stewart and Joseph Alsop. He was silent to an astonishing degree, and he seemed completely casual in making assignments; I remember no word of commendation or criticism, though on one painful occasion he gave me advice. Yet he got things done, and he evoked devoted loyalty from his associates. Moreover, in his own silent way he showed appreciation of work well done. He was as close to perfect efficiency as any administrator I have known. I never saw him hurry, or observed him idle. His judgments were calm —and sound.

He gave me a wholly free hand in my assignment. I traveled to cities that had made a success, sent out hundreds of questionnaires, and wrote a small volume of about 150 pages which set forth the procedures in detail. The entire job, including publication of the book, was completed in about three months. It was no literary masterpiece, but it remained, so far as I know, the only full-length discussion of the matter until the Second World War. It was indubitably the reason I was appointed, with Winthrop W. Aldrich, Chester I. Barnard, Ralph Hayes, and Gerard Swope, to organize the National War Fund during the Second World War.

Mr. Alsop supported me vigorously in controversial matters. Passages in the report were displeasing to some of the officers of the Red Cross in Washington, three of whom (all personal friends later) came to protest my views before the Council of Defense. After full consideration the Council overruled their objections, but an incident associated with the episode made a permanent impression. After the session had adjourned, Justice George W. Wheeler of the Connecticut Supreme Court met me in the hall. To me he was an awesome figure, stern, ascetic, and acerb. He stopped and said, "We had to back you up because you were right; but don't be right in such an irritating way again."

The book had one wholly unexpected result: it made me an "expert" on fund raising. The word belongs in quotations. My *expertise* was superficial to a degree; it was based on observation and description rather than mature experience. Nevertheless, the reputation of being especially competent in that field had a decisive influence on my future career.

When the War Chest assignment was concluded, I was

made assistant manager of the Council and had the benefit of daily association with Mr. Alsop. One incident illustrates his methods. It was suggested that the governor should send a letter to high school students urging them to stay in school and neither volunteer for the armed services too soon nor seek work in war factories. Successively the presidents of Yale, Wesleyan, and the Connecticut State College at Storrs were requested to draft the letter. Successively, after deliberating a week or two, they declined, to Mr. Alsop's disgust, and he decided to abandon the project. At noontime I drafted a letter, left it on his desk, and heard no comment from him. Two days later I asked what was in process in the duplicating room; it was my letter, signed by the governor. It was a silent form of praise that was far more potent than any words could have been.

It also gave me some insight into how public documents are prepared. My education in this respect was advanced when the governor, at Mr. Alsop's suggestion, asked me to draft a portion of his second inaugural for his "consideration." For many years I kept the newspaper clippings which commented upon "how characteristic" it was of the governor to say some things I had written with no consultation with him or anyone else.

My political education was proceeding, but not fast enough. The end of the war brought a prompt demand for the end of war work; it was suggested that the Council of Defense should immediately disband. This would leave many good programs without leadership for peace time. Clearly, it seemed to me, there should be a period of transition. So I drafted a proposed editorial and gave it to the representative of one of the Hartford papers for the consideration of its editor. It appeared as a news item—and it was far from news. The rival paper spotted it and suggested editorially that this was a trick by Mr. Alsop to continue to exercise his unusual powers. I told him I would deny he had anything to do with it, which was true. He did not forbid me—that would have been out of character; but he did advise me to let the matter drop. Of course I knew better, and issued the denial. This led to a new outburst; the paper asserted that when caught he fobbed responsibility off onto a subordinate. I learned, at last, and to his cost, that it does no good to deny what a paper wants to believe.

The experience in Hartford had been worth while. It had vastly broadened my acquaintance. Academic circles tend to be closed circles; without some special stimulus there is little occasion to widen one's contacts or outlook. I had learned a lot about practical politics; my job was nonpolitical and there was no politics in the Council of Defense, but, being attached to the governor's office, I necessarily saw a good deal of political action at close range. Thereafter my teaching of political "science"—a misnomer—took on a different cast.

It was my first real contact with men of large affairs. My strongly democratic home training had prevented me from regarding them as in any way superior people; the idea of a privileged class was not part of my equipment. But I was definitely impressed by the size of their activities and the range of their powers. In actual dealings, however, they proved not to be "tycoons" or "big shots" or any of the other mythical constructs so common to our daily speech. To meet with them day after day and find them ordinary people like my faculty colleagues, and as easy to work with, cured me of that kind of awe so easily conjured up when contacts with prominent leaders are rare or distant.

I had served my apprenticeship in administration with an expert, a man of the highest ideals who never put expediency before principle. My eyes were opened even wider than before to the value of expert secretarial work; because of the splendid organization of the reference and stenographic departments I was able to write at a pace which would have been impossible in academic life.

I had learned a great deal about public relations, partly through observation of men skilled in its techniques, but even more by hard—not to say painful—experience. Furthermore, I was offered various jobs at three and four times the college salary I would receive. They were interesting and challenging opportunities quite apart from the financial lure. Making up my mind to decline and go back to teaching now that Wesleyan needed my services meant a new and final commitment to academic life.

Scarcely had I returned to the classroom, however, when another interruption occurred. The war had disrupted the colleges. Rising costs had made them poorer than ever; it is hard to appreciate, with our current standards, how poverty-stricken they had always been. For the first time the war and its consequences had brought them into competition with industry for scientists, economists, and other academic talent. Sheer necessity produced the greatest effort at money raising that American higher education had yet seen. For the most part it was directed by a new group of professionals, men who reshaped completely the traditional methods of "begging" for money. My own college set out to raise three million dollars, triple any goal it had ever set before.

Begging was the president's business, and there was none better at it than Dr. Shanklin. But for a campaign of such unexampled magnitude he needed an organizer. That was a talent which he lacked. It was suggested that I should be given a new leave of absence to undertake the task. Was I not an "expert"—the man who wrote the book on fund raising? Had I not had administrative and organizing experience?

However, there were serious drawbacks to the proposition. My relations with the president were personally friendly. I was still "Hennery." But I disapproved of him academically. He was not a scholar; he had none of the tastes, habits, methods, or procedures of a scholar. He could not be called an intellectual; his reading was not of that sort; he was not a man of ideas. He did not know one end of a curriculum from another, and he made little or no contribution to thought about the course of study. I doubt he could have evaluated a high school transcript to determine whether a candidate should be admitted as a freshman. His ideas of student discipline and mine were often in conflict—conflict that was sometimes vigorous in tone as well as substance. I did not regard him as a good administrator; he did not know how to use a secretary efficiently. In short, despite pleasant personal relationships, I felt strongly that from an academic standpoint the college should have had quite another type of leader. If the decision had been left entirely to me I would certainly have declined the proposed assignment.

Faculty persuasion, which amounted to pressure, tipped the scale the other way. One of the senior professors, a really great teacher, pointed out the desperate need for salary increases. He had what New Englanders used to call "a competence" and so was not directly involved. He reminded me of what everyone knew, that the president could not do it alone, that the trustees were not giving him strong backing, and that the faculty would suffer the consequences of any failure of the campaign. He felt that in view of my experience it was my duty to undertake the task. Other members of the faculty added their words, but his were decisive, and I accepted the appointment.

It made me the direct and personal assistant of a man whom I liked, but with whom I was in vigorous disagreement. Looking back, I can now see clearly that it was at this time that my preference for an academic man in the college presidency hardened into a profound conviction. I cannot deny that ministers, lawyers, military officers, bankers, businessmen, and others have occasionally done well. But the sound rule is that the president should be a scholar; all the other essential attributes should be present, but secondary. Fifty years of first-hand observation confirm me in that judgment.

I was resigned to a collaboration that was unwelcome, but I was totally unprepared for a flank attack. After being granted leave of absence, I turned over my notes and my personal library to a hastily appointed substitute. He had just arrived from Europe and had neither books nor any necessity for teaching. When the road back to my classroom was completely blocked, I was invited to New York to discuss my new work with the chairman of the board of trustees.

He began by expressing his regret at the interruption to my teaching as well as the dislocation of my persistent efforts at research. He expressed the hope that, far from exacerbating this latter difficulty, my new assignment could be made to advance the project upon which, for some years, I had worked at every available moment. The smooth expressions of friendliness and interest in my welfare flowed on—suspiciously long, coming from a man who had never before taken a perceptible interest in my progress.

At last the corner of the monologue was turned and he came to the point. The trustees wanted a change in the presidency; a successful campaign would defeat their desire. Therefore, the campaign should be made to fail. He suggested that I go back to Middletown, make a few gestures toward setting up a campaign, but bend my real energies to research. Success with a scholarly book, coinciding with a change in administration, might result in turning the attention of a selection committee my way.

In all the years since I have never forgotten the headache that interview induced. I wondered if I would live to reach Grand Central Station from lower Broadway. My position seemed completely hopeless. I must work intimately with a man of whom I disapproved. It had now been made abundantly clear that there would be no cooperation in the project from leading trustees, who, to give them full credit, were themselves excellent money raisers. The appointment could be a steppingstone to an old ambition only on terms that would prove me unfit for the reward.

With these bleak prospects, we closed our house in Middletown; my wife and children went to Springfield to live with her mother and father. I took a room and also an office on the top floor of the old Manhattan Hotel at Madison and Forty-Second and began seeking out alumni who were ready to work and to give. The campaign got under way. This transparent answer to the proposals that had been made to me by the chairman of the board brought warnings far more explicit than his. A trustee whose friendship I could not question, a high church official, former president of a great university, took me in hand; he sought to persuade me not to wreck my career by fighting a battle that could not be won. In response, I tried to make clear my view that hiring and firing presidents were responsibilities of the trustees, that they had no right to use me for a pawn in the effort to achieve an end they desired but would not face directly.

We parted without personal rancor but also without compromise; none was offered on either side. However, he was one of a few who continued to treat me kindly. Another stands out in the same group. He was perhaps the bitterest critic of the president, the most eager to see him out of office. He made no concealment of his attitude; indeed he was forthright in his readiness to take full responsibility for direct action. He called me on the telephone, invited me to Delmonico's for dinner and on to a Broadway show. He was blunt: "I will do everything possible to prevent the success of your task, but I will not be a party to abusing you personally." Such friendliness was so rare among members of the governing board of the college that it was profoundly appreciated. When we met, by tacit agreement we never discussed college business, but he made my exceedingly lonely life more bearable.

The campaign went a good deal better than might have been expected. I learned a lot from other campaign directors, for nearly every Eastern institution had a "drive" on with headquarters in New York. For the first time, in any large way, professionals were employed to direct them. In such company I was a tyro indeed; several, like John Price Jones, generously gave me advice and assistance. Moreover, nearly all alumni were cooperative, and the "drive" moved forward.

So far as the effect upon my subsequent career was concerned, the really significant aspect of the experience was in gaining a new perspective on college presidents. Intimate friends of my chief were Donald J. Cowling, then in the first vigorous stages of making Carleton one of the best colleges in America, and J. H. T. Main, the distinguished president of Grinnell. They seemed to spend a good share of their time in New York, looking for money, of course. Inevitably, I heard the shop talk of both the Eastern seaboard and the Middle West. I gained some insight into the arduous character of money raising, its tremendous drain upon the physical and nervous energy of presidents.

This was dramatized for me one evening before I knew the men very well. After a singularly taxing and exhausting day, President Main said to me, "I think I will commit suicide." His bearing, his voice and manner alarmed me, and as quickly as possible I reported the remark to my own president. He and Dr. Cowling joined Dr. Main and set out to cheer him up. They chose a method that struck me then as a most unlikely therapy for acute depression: they went off together to a seance! He came back much refreshed.

The three presidents drove themselves unmercifully. I worked to the limit of my endurance but never seemed able to approximate their exertions. It told upon the health of my chief. He was white, drawn, was losing weight, and spent many sleepless nights. When I met him for breakfast in the Transportation Club on the top floor of the Manhattan his appearance was alarming. The heart trouble that was to end his life was all too apparent. Again and again I begged him to rest, to relax, to slow the pace. As well talk to the wind; in a few moments he was off on that endless round of calls asking for money.

None of the experiences of this strenuous year altered my conviction that a college president should be a scholar, but they did convince me that there was a prior and still more important quality: a commitment to higher education which no discouragement could shake—indeed, with which nothing could successfully compete. All these men with whom my lot was cast had that quality to the uttermost. My own president was almost literally killing himself by overexertion in a cause which engaged his whole energy. He was an innocent in politics, a tyro in philosophy, unread in literature, and to him science was a blank page.

He had no interests, no ambitions, no desires that I could discover save to do with all his heart and mind and will what his office required.

A second thing I learned as I came to know these presidents better: few men have all the talents—very few. Most have limited abilities. No one whom I have ever known could do all the things expected of a college president and do all of them well. Often a man is suited to part of the task, that part which is most urgent at the moment of his appointment. My president had been elected when the college was small and seemed to be getting smaller. My class was the smallest, and probably the poorest, in many years. Deficits had become chronic; salaries were wretched. The best professors were steadily tempted to go elsewhere; when they did not leave it was some family tie, some regional attachment which held them. When the new president talked of limiting the student body to five hundred a smile, not too well concealed, went around; nobody believed he could get five hundred. In short, what the college most needed at that moment was a man with the gifts of a promoter, who could get students and raise money.

By good fortune academic standards were safe in the hands of the faculty; even the curriculum could be revised with a minimum of departmental logrolling. But no one, save the president, could do the promotional work which was the first requisite. And he did it. The student body went up to five hundred—and past it. The first million-dollar campaign succeeded; in the new campaign sights were raised to three million. Moreover, he got strong men to join the board of trustees; it was the men he recruited who ultimately put the institution in as sound financial condition as any in the entire country.

The trouble with my chief, I decided, in the light of what I was learning in New York, was that he had succeeded.

When he came to the office he was just what was most desperately needed, a promoter. Success in promotion made the other qualities which the new situation demanded conspicuous by their absence. Two episodes illustrate the point.

He was asked to speak in a neighboring city during "education week." He called me into his office and said he had to accept; there was no available excuse which he could offer. But he had nothing to say; his candor was breathtaking. He explained that he had devoted so much time and energy to promotion that he had not kept up with either reading or thinking about educational problems. He asked me to prepare a speech so that, at the last moment, he could send me as a substitute with the best excuse he could muster. That episode stayed with me during thirty years as a college president; it drove me to the conviction that I must read widely outside my own professional field; it made me ration my efforts in such a way as to leave time for thought about education.

Another incident arising out of concentration upon promotion was equally impressive to me. A group of faculty—who knew nothing of the problem the president had tackled in 1909, but all about his deficiencies in 1920—was denouncing him for making unwarranted statements, "promises" these men called them, which he had not fulfilled. The denunciations became heated until one turned to the short and ugly: "The president is a liar!" Whereupon the senior professor, a slight, wiry man, not over five feet five, with a quavering voice and a tendency to say "ooh" as he formed sentences, came to the defense of the president. It was the most extraordinary plea of confession and avoidance I have ever heard.

"The president," he intoned, "is not a li-ar. To be a li-ar one must consciously deviate from the truth. It is clear that what he said was inaccurate, but he has been saying these things so long that he has convinced himself and does not perceive their untruth." This could have been the origin of the wisecrack that the duty of the dean is to make the college what the president has long asserted it already is. When I myself held office I found how extremely hard it is to say what has to be said for promotional purposes without making dreams, hopes, prophecies sound like specific promises or even current attainments.

The last lesson of my work in New York has all the elements of farce, but truth could never prevail over myth. I attained a false but brilliant "success" without a stroke of work. One morning at breakfast I asked "Prexy" if he knew William F. Armstrong; he said he did. So I inquired if we could approach him for a gift. He replied that we were in Mr. Armstrong's will but he was not to be approached about money. When I asked what we might expect, the answer was "about $100,000." Whereupon I put an end to my teasing questions and told him that Mr. Armstrong had died, left a bequest of $100,000, and made the college residuary legatee in an amount of about a million. I got credit for that million; no explanation I offered made any difference; I was a successful money raiser!

At the end of my leave I withdrew from the campaign, which was already well organized, and was replaced by a professional firm. The next year was spent in research, catching up on work so often interrupted and long overdue. During those months I found so much satisfaction in study in the State Department archives that I was prepared to spend my life in teaching and writing. When, at last, I returned once more to the classroom it was with zest beyond any I had ever known before. I poured my energies into writing new lectures in a new field. The bitter experience of the financial campaign, the acid comment of a trustee that my "success" had prolonged the term of the president, all but cured me of any youthful ambition for top administration. College administration had lost its glamor; it would need very little to sour me on it completely.

That reaction proceeded apace. After the campaign the president was given leave of absence for a year. In his stead we had an acting president, a distinguished New York lawyer, whose wife was wealthy. Socially it was a gala year. The president's house was made attractive with beautiful furniture and staffed with servants; a series of dinners and teas and concerts made the campus lively indeed. The contrast with the efforts of the president's wife to run the great ark of a house upon a pitifully small salary and with no servants at all was striking, but not encouraging from a faculty point of view.

The choice of the acting president was transparently sentimental. He had been born on the campus, the son of Wesleyan's second president, and had been a trustee for over forty years. He was a true intellectual, a man of grace and charm, but not experienced academically. As a consequence his ideas on curriculum, on discipline, on all matters academic were those of an amateur. It made the faculty fearful lest when a new presidential appointment came to be made we should have someone selected for his social standing, his business experience, or some other quality not central to the task.

The acting president found his office cramped and inconvenient—as it was. So the faculty meeting room was redecorated for the president's office, and his former quarters turned over to a secretary. Portraits of all past presidents were collected from various buildings about the campus, cleaned, and hung in the great room. It was a beautiful place—two stories high, with magnificent windows, and admirable proportions.

In the course of that year my wife and I purchased an old house, built in 1787, and remodeled it, doing as little violence to its antiquity as possible while repairing the ravages of time and neglect. It fronted on the street that passed the side of the president's mansion and overlooked the mansion's backyard. It was only a step away from my pleasant office in the oldest college building and from my classroom in the newest. In the midst of the reconstruction a telegram arrived, asking me to accept the presidency of a small Western college. The telegram I sent in response was an explicit negative. It offered concrete evidence that I was content to settle down to my professorship as a career.

Nevertheless, the climax of disillusion was yet to come. The acting president moved out. Van loads of elegant furniture and beautiful objects departed. Into the rather bare spaces came the normal tenant—or rather his wife; he was said to be in New York. The president's wife was one of the really lovely characters whom I have known—gentle, industrious, gracious, thoughtful, one could pile up adjectives indefinitely without doing violence to the facts. In all the rough-and-tumble of college politics and the devious machinations of trustees I never heard a word of criticism of her from anyone.

When she appeared in her yard for a moment, I rushed over, full of gladness at her return and enthusiasm about prospects for the future. She greeted me warmly, but my ebullience kept me from observing the tension in her manner. After questions about her year of leave, I urged her to come and see her husband's new office, with the preparation of which I had had a small but enthusiastic part. She demurred, but nothing could restrain my insistence. Arrived at the office I descanted upon its charm and appropriateness, called attention to the portraits, and then planted my foot firmly in my mouth. Pointing to the paneled walls I remarked: "There is not much room to hang any more presidents."

At that *gaffe* her self-control snapped and in a storm of tears she answered, "They are hanging another right now, Henry." The controlling group of trustees had finally abandoned artifice and indirection and asked the president to resign. Not many years before I would have hailed the act, for I was acutely aware of his academic deficiencies. But living in New York and participating daily in his labors had shown me the other side of the coin. I had come to know his utter devotion, his unselfish toil, and his personal charm. I felt he was entitled to the very few years that remained before normal retirement.

Not only were my sympathies deeply engaged, my sense of justice and fair dealing was outraged. The trustees had chosen him, and he had done what he was brought in from Iowa to do—to change the rhythm of the institution, to build up the student body, the plant, and the endowment. He had even attained the height of one prominent trustee's ambition—the college dinner was held in the Astor hotel, with tuxedoes required. This trivial snobbishness was bitter as gall to an academic.

Dismay and distress at the tragic event were enough to quench the last spark of my ambition to be a college president. What a contrast was this hole-in-the-corner closing of an administration with its beginning amid pomp and circumstance, graced by the President of the United States. I had been "on the inside" at the start and was again "on the inside" at the end.

If emotional response had not proved enough to cure me of an early infatuation, the events immediately following taught me a lesson I have never forgotten. The dismissed president had no other calling. It was far too late for him to return to the ministry. He could not teach. His business experience had been negligible; the whole apparatus of college budgets, of budget control, of "management" had not been developed. Academic procedures and business methods were as far apart as the East from the West. And since his salary had been wretched, he had not been able to save; provision for his "retirement" was conspicuously inadequate. So a trustee helped him get a job as a real estate salesman in a big new "development."

What his feelings may well have been I can imagine. But I never heard a whimper or a complaint from him. He turned to his new task with furious energy and complete absorption—and died of a heart attack in the subway station at Grand Central within a year. The whole tragic episode was not calculated to leave much glamor in the office of college president, or to maintain a young man's enthusiasm for such a career.

Meanwhile the vice-president served as acting president at Wesleyan and the trustees set out on their quest for a new executive. Such an interregnum, even under the best of circumstances, is always a tense time for a faculty. All important decisions tend to be postponed so as not to "commit" the new administrator to a course of which he might not approve. Rumors fly in the best classical tradition, and the names of "candidates" are bandied about, seldom with any real foundation. In this instance the tension was greater than normal; it always is when a president has been displaced before his time.

To that circumstance was added a fact soon made very plain: the trustees wanted no help—called "interference"—from the faculty. Some were rather candid about their feelings. They believed that the faculty had had "too much to say" about how the college was run. To men who had little contact with day-to-day collegiate affairs such a conclusion was natural. For two decades the presidency had not supplied strong internal leadership. A sick and tired man held office at first; there had been at least three acting presidents for longer or shorter periods; and the administration just ended had been devoted to promotion of student attendance and finances. Even this last program had been interrupted while the president went overseas for war work.

Inevitably curriculum, discipline, indeed the whole domestic program, fell into faculty hands, for want of others if for no better reason. Just as the trustees were tired of a promoter, so also they were tired of faculty dominance. Some of them said bluntly they wanted a new president who would "run the college" and "put the faculty in its place"—a position not very well-defined in their minds, but definitely in the background. In any event, there was virtually no consultation even with the acting president; he was tarred with the "faculty" brush. As this became evident faculty concern increased. They well knew that though a president did not have power to run the place alone he could be a barrier to progress. A man brought in with the purpose of curtailing faculty control could have a negative effect upon the educational program.

As suddenly as the old administration was terminated, the new one was announced after a year-long wait. It was revealed under equally unpromising auspices. At noon on the day of the annual Williams football game, telephone calls summoned the faculty to a meeting "right after the game." All the members were in their places promptly, and a trustee announced that a new president had been chosen. He told very little about the man, but spent considerable time explaining how to pronounce his name correctly. At any other moment it would have seemed a hilarious farce; to a group to whom the substance of the announcement meant so much, the heavy accent upon the irrelevant was anything but funny.

Who's Who, to which we resorted, made it clear that the appointee had a sound education, the "union card" of scholarship—a Ph.D., and was experienced in several phases of college work, including that of being president of a strong Midwest college. Only one member of the faculty seemed to know him well; his descriptions were not flattering, but he was known by us all to be colorful in expression, sometimes at the risk of making a caricature rather than a portrait.

My own feeling was one of relief that the suspense was over, without a trace of personal disappointment. The leading group in the trustees had made it plain that failure to sabotage the financial campaign had put me in their bad graces. The relief was short-lived. I received a letter from the trustee who had made the announcement to the faculty stating that he did not like the expression on my face! In retrospect I can see all the elements of humor in the situation. But I was in no mood to accept a rebuke or to laugh it off. My letter in response made that plain with a great deal of emphasis. I was a professor with tenure, attending to my teaching and research; it was none of a trustee's business to attempt to read my mind by some interpretation of a facial expression. The answer to my letter was a contribution to heat without light. And so it went, the letters from each to the other becoming more absurd and irrelevant. A sense of humor—the essence of reason—was totally banished. Finally the correspondence ended from exhaustion of epithets.

A less promising introduction to the new administrator would be difficult to conceive, for he had been told of the whole affair. Nevertheless, expectations of fireworks were defeated. The new president came. We were neighbors. His wife and mine had been in college together, and, while not close, they were friendly. His children and mine were of an age and swapped the boasts and threats appropriate to four- and six-year-olds. And I was made one of the two marshals for the inauguration, being deputy to the chemistry professor, an intimate friend. As a consequence we were in the president's office many times. The formula was always the same: "Good morning, gentlemen, what is the problem?" When the matter was before him, his next response was standard: "What do you advise?" Usually he accepted promptly; when he modified or altered the proposed course it was with tact and sound reason. A more harmonious relationship would be difficult to imagine.

Suddenly I discovered that my name was on three lists of prospects for college presidencies. I suspected some of the trustees had sought thus to "promote" me out, and I went to New York to consult the former university president whose earlier advice I had declined to follow. My question was simple: which of the three was the most plastic, the one most ready for action. He discussed the three and said Lawrence, in Wisconsin. Moreover, he felt that if the opportunity came I should take it—a clear hint.

On the morning of June 5, 1925, I participated—again "on the inside"—at the inauguration of the new president. In the midst of the luncheon I left to go to Appleton to see Lawrence and talk with the trustees. It was my first experience with this ritual and it left an indelible impression upon me.

The faculty committee sent to meet me in Chicago missed me, but we made contact in Milwaukee and had three or four hours of talk on the train. Arriving in Appleton I was the guest of a leading trustee and was shown around. There seemed to be some indefinable effort to keep me under strict surveillance. There was an atmosphere of excitement and a good deal of whispering in corners that did not relate to me but piqued my curiosity. Also there was a pungent smell in the air. So during the baccalaureate sermon I escaped from the chapel, alone at last, and followed my nose. It led me straight to the men's dormitory, where there had been a serious fire the night before my arrival. At that moment I began what later became characteristic: I went through the building from cellar to garret to see at first hand what had happened and what should be done to prevent a recurrence.

The talks with trustees and faculty were elaborately casual. No one wanted to commit himself in any way. I learned, through someone's inadvertence, that I was not the first choice; the post had been offered to a clergyman with university experience. He had declined, making it clear that he had episcopal ambitions—which, I am happy to record, were ultimately fulfilled.

After three days I returned to Middletown and reported upon my expedition to President McConaughy. Up to that time our relations had been not only correct but cordial; nevertheless they were essentially impersonal and official. Now they were the reverse. He told me candidly that some trustees, disappointed by the success of the financial campaign, had advised him to induce me to resign, or if need be to fire me, which he knew and his advisers should have known was *ultra vires*. He told me, too, that he saw no reason we could not work together in harmony. Indeed he offered me one of the "bonus" salaries which the trustees had just established. I made it plain that such an arrangement would bring discord into a harmonious faculty, and that acceptance of such a benefit would cost me more in my relations with my colleagues than the money would bring.

Nevertheless the conversation brought complete relaxation of any tensions which might have existed on either side. Shortly thereafter came a formal invitation to go to Lawrence as president. We loved our home, only recently acquired and rebuilt; there were no less than ninety rose bushes of every variety in our garden, a gift from a student. Our faculty friends meant the world to us; they were genial, stimulating, and good fun. My teaching was absorbing and exciting, for the students were well chosen and responsive. Research, often discouraged in colleges, was promoted and the library was almost lavish with assistance. Salaries were good, as academic salaries went, and gave promise of further improvement.

Twice I started to the telephone to send a telegram declining. Twice my wife called me back and advised me to reflect upon the matter longer. She was not eager to go, and her family, who lived in Springfield, were opposed; but she knew it was a definitive decision and felt it should be unhurried. Delay brought the president of the Lawrence board of trustees to Middletown, and he made it all sound so attractive that on July 4, 1925—my thirty-sixth birthday—we accepted.

Inevitably there was an afterclap of farce. One of the Wesleyan trustees had been elected lieutenant governor many years before and was made governor through the death of the governor in an automobile accident. With the heartlessness of the very young we all called him, during our college years, "His Accidency." He belonged to the old school, was as prim, precise, and proper as only the old school could be, and as conservative as a Connecticut Republican of the classic tradition. He met me in the street: "What's this I hear about going to Wisconsin? It's a great mistake. If you go way out there among the Indians you will be buried and never heard from again." To one born in Wyoming, Wisconsin did not seem that far away. The episode gave a light touch to the emotional wrench of leaving our home, our friends, and the almost idyllic—but very strenuous—life of a teacher.

My apprenticeship was over; I was now to be a journeyman in the college president's trade. I knew even then—and much more acutely later—that I was no master of the art.

Two basic skills were mine: teaching and research. Both seemed essential to me then, and increasingly so ever since. In one, research, I had been carefully trained. College seminars had supplied the elements of investigation; at graduate school, intensive instruction and practice had carried me forward; while I taught at Wesleyan research was a major activity. Teaching, on the other hand, had been learned mostly by observation and hard experience; at no time did I have any formal instruction. My college teachers were as various in their methods, their manner, and their matter as men could be. Graduate work revealed the same endless diversity in method and mood.

I concluded that teaching was an art, and an art it is. At Harvard I taught in the capacity of a "section hand" in a large course given by Dean Charles Homer Haskins. His lectures were models of form, substance, and clarity. In the weekly discussions of the course program he gave many informal suggestions. When I began to teach my own courses I naturally turned to the lecture method; it was what I had experienced for the most part as a student both in college and graduate school. The process was carried to its ultimate absurdity, however, when I stood to give a formal lecture course to three students, one of whom had been a classmate in college but had dropped out for a few years because of family difficulties. It was hard to be dignified when one of the three students greeted me each day with "Hello, Hank."

In some courses in government (in which I had no training whatever) I tried the method of discussion. Having had little experience either in observing others or as a participant, I found the process difficult. Ultimately, I turned whenever possible to informal give and take by which the student is drawn out, and both his knowledge and his deficiencies made startlingly clear not only to the teacher but —much more important—to him.

It may seem odd to stress these phases of my apprenticeship when there was to be so little opportunity to apply either the one or the other during the years of administrative work. The reason for the emphasis is that both profoundly affected my attitudes as a college president. A good teacher is a prize, a great teacher a jewel beyond price. Unless one has taught, and has had first-hand experience with the problems, it is hard to appreciate how exacting are the demands of good teaching, how arduous is the self-discipline necessary to avoid easing off and slacking preparation in the belief (or hope) that the students will not know the difference. They may not detect such tactics at once, but sooner or later they will. Therefore the teaching background was invaluable, however scant the opportunity to unite instruction with administration.

Research was just as important as background for administration. Relative to their responsibilities and obligations, colleges are poor. There is always a temptation to "save money" on activities that do not appear to help the students directly. Research is such an activity; it "cuts into teaching time" and energy. If it results in publication, few read the papers or books—the students never. The subject matter appears to trustees irrelevant and immaterial, however competent. "What's the good of it?" is a common question from the "practical" businessman. But if a president has done research he knows how vital it is and why the process is so slow and the published result often so apparently slender. He will not be tempted to weigh the papers by bulk or to count their number; in the fields of his own competence he will judge the quality of the man by his work; in fields outside his competence he will seek the counsel of those whose standing is incontestable.

Moreover he will have come to know, at first hand, how much research activity contributes to the freshness of teaching—and to its authority. In this context authority is a vital word. When the students discover that the professor publishes, and gets good reviews, their receptiveness to his instruction is heightened. Learning is a voluntary act; the attitude of the students is decisive, and particularly so at the higher levels. The reputation of a professor profoundly affects their readiness to respond to his instruction.

By the time I became a college president, I had heard many times all the arguments designed to prove that good teaching and good research seldom go together. My own observation and experience convinced me that generally the reverse is true: they complement each other.

Beyond teaching and research, my apprenticeship included familiarity with academic protocol. Participation in two presidential inaugurations, once as an undergraduate press officer and once as deputy chief marshal, plus a long series of convocations and commencements had shown me the whole bag of tricks. From some points of view academic protocol is as trivial as diplomatic precedence—even more so. But so are all the customary forms of everyday courtesy—tipping the hat, shaking hands, and all the rest. Constant repetition of familiar formulas make them seem hackneyed; any analysis of academic gowns, hoods, and hats is a weariness. Yet I could remember my own thrill, as an undergraduate, at the pageantry. Moreover, I had watched students and parents—and alumni—manifest great emotion in what were, to them, unusual circumstances.

Over the many years of reenacting the ceremonials at convocations and commencements I came to appreciate the feelings of the actor who has played the same role so often he could do it in his sleep, yet puts his whole art into each performance because it is the "first night" for nearly all his audience. The teacher must remember that the new class cannot begin where he left off with its predecessors; he must again produce the effect of novelty where novelty is long since lost to him. In the same spirit a president must breathe something of reality into academic pageantry which familiarity makes personally boresome. An early knowledge of protocol is most helpful in this endeavor.

As part of my apprenticeship I had come to know how students select their courses and their fields of concentration. The irresponsibility with which I had approached the matter myself was still fresh in memory. I had put off selecting a "major" until the last moment. When I went to the study of the German professor, intending to "sign up" with him, he was out, and I did not know where to find him. So I proceeded from the third floor to the first, and approached the history professor's lair. But I knew he snarled when he said "come in," and I was not ready to face his sarcastic barbs. After studying the ground glass of his door for a few moments, I climbed to the second floor and signed up with the gentle, genial professor of English literature, a "decision" I never regretted. To this day when I hear over-pretentious discussions of "the process of decision-making" that episode comes to mind.

Beyond memory, I had experience. As a young faculty member I had the task, with the aid of a good secretary, of registering the whole junior class. It required checking their choices of concentration, their eligibility for the courses they had elected both within and outside that field. Literally hundreds were as casual in their approach, and as unstable in their reasons for those choices as I had been at their time of life. Moreover, those who selected the "easy" courses stood out like sore thumbs; the motives of those who jealously guarded their week ends from the intrusion of Saturday classes were as naked as a needle. Those who were "scutting" Phi Beta Kappa and shaped their programs to that end were vastly more obvious about it than they ever dreamed.

In short, to register a class where "critical" decisions had to be made was an eye opener. Never again could I get unduly disturbed by the "irresponsibility" of students, or their "instability." Those are manifestations of the process of growing up; some grow slowly, some almost too fast, and some not at all. A college president who has romantic or abstract or unreal convictions about students and their selection of courses is headed for disillusionment.

Discipline was another aspect of administration that had come within my experience. Service upon the committee on administration revealed both the serious and the comic sides of academic "justice." The dean, who was the dominant figure and a great wit, delighted and infuriated me. On one occasion a handsome lad—a brilliant student, president of the student body, a good halfback, a winning sprinter, and the leader of the glee club—committed some minor but annoying academic sin. Argument was long and loud, one faculty member extoling his virtues, the next saying he must not take advantage of those to break college rules. Finally, the dean, weary of the straw threshed long after the grain was pulped, burst out, "Mr. President, I move we kill him and stuff him, on the ground he will never be so beautiful again." It ended a silly discussion.

On another occasion I came under the whip of his wit. A college infirmary with a physician in charge had just been established; every student was supposed to get sick excuses from the doctor. The dean did not much care for rules himself, so when some boys came to his counter with inflamed eyes he promptly diagnosed their trouble as pink eye and told them not to return to the campus until fully cured. It never entered his mind that their illness occurred on Friday. A wave of merriment swept across the campus; the boys had put tobacco juice in their eyes; after being excused by the dean, they washed them out with boric acid and took off for Smith College and all the joys it held.

Those of us who had long wanted a real health service were outraged. At the next faculty meeting I undertook to rebuke the dean for his trespass upon the duties of the health officer. I had prepared carefully and made my comments as strong as possible. The dean, in his capacity as secretary of the faculty, sat beside the president. He was utterly British in temper and lounged in his place with the same disregard for posture and decorum as the occupants of the Front Bench in Parliament. He was sitting on the small of his back with his knees propped against the edge of the table before him. When my diatribe was over the president turned and asked if he had any comment. He dropped his feet to the floor, sat up part way, and said, "It is my considered judgment, Mr. President, that if a boy can spit in his own eye he deserves a week-end vacation." In the gale of laughter my point was lost, but the dean was more careful to send "ailing" students to the doctor thereafter.

The committee on administration also checked the observance of academic rules. Thus I learned the almost inevitable tendency of the scholastic bureaucracy to tithe with mint, anise, and cummin, while neglecting the weightier matters of the law. Experience in that group colored indelibly my approach to registrars. It was an essential part of a presidential apprenticeship.

The curriculum committee was the second "key" body of the faculty upon which I was called to serve. Before doing so I led a revolt against it. A group of enthusiastic "young Turks" developed a scheme for promoting independent work on the part of the best students, inducting them into the joys of individual learning and the excitement that comes from the pursuit of knowledge. The plan was referred to the curriculum committee who decided to smother it with a resolution praising the idea and its authors, but postponing action pending "further study." The report was obviously the kiss of death. In the last meeting of the year I moved to lay the report on the table, approve the program in principle, and instruct the committee to bring in a specific proposal for putting it into practice. The motion lost by a single vote—that of a friend of mine who thought I was "fooling." Nevertheless, the committee did bring in an acceptable plan early in the next year.

Making a curriculum has always reminded me of a story my father told me long before I began to teach. He seldom told stories, and I have forgotten all but two. In this instance the county agent was pleading with an inefficient farmer to take a short course with the extension division of the state college in order to improve the productivity of his farm. The agent argued and pleaded, he used economic and social arguments, all to no avail. Exasperated, he finally shouted, "Give me one good reason why you won't take the course." The farmer replied: "I ain't farming half as well as I know how now; what good would it be to learn more things I won't do?"

Curriculums in American colleges are not half as good as members of the faculty know how to make them. Departmental satrapies, personal prepossessions and antipathies, logrolling, petty politics—these and a dozen others of the less admirable aspects of academic life account for the complicated hodgepodge that goes by the name of curriculum. The word means "race course"; they make it an obstacle race. Long before I had administrative responsibility I learned that faculties are not "curricularizing" half as well as they know how.

Two of the ablest scholars and teachers, colleagues in a department later split into two, never spoke to each other or appeared together save in faculty meetings. If any curricular change was suggested, the support of one guaranteed the opposition of the other. Some of the best debating I ever heard was between these two antagonists in sessions of the faculty. Their courtesy was elaborate, they referred to each other only in indirect discourse and in the most flattering terms—edged with irony. But their discussions of the point at issue were models of their kind, and almost always a perfect standoff. The result was no action. If one was silent, both were silent, and a result was achieved. They epitomized those personal currents that flow through faculties and affect curricular reform so disastrously.

I learned the hard way how much energy, patience, and persistence even the most modest step in the improvement of the curriculum requires. And of one other thing I had an inkling but not full realization, namely, that reform easily exhausts the energies of its proponents and that the stubborn, silent, but destructive effect of passive resistance is continuous, pervasive, and insidious. A change voted is merely a challenge to resistance; the vote is preliminary to the real battle.

My apprenticeship touched also the ever present, sensitive problems of personnel. Faculty appointments, and more particularly faculty promotions and the grant of tenure, had to pass through a "president's advisory committee." Most of its members were senior members of the faculty, but I attained "seniority" fairly young, having been dropped from the Young Faculty Club at thirty because I had been made a full professor. When I left Wesleyan six years later

I was fourteenth in order of seniority in a faculty of about eighty. My service on the advisory committee was therefore not so extraordinary as it seems in retrospect.

Nevertheless, it forced me to form judgments about men older than myself, and taught me how dauntingly serious a responsibility that is. It also taught me that a committee is not a good instrument for final judgment. In that instance its "advice" could not be contravened; it was in fact, if not in form, decisive. "My department" and its needs constantly intruded upon judgment regarding an individual. The social relationships among the wives became involved. Dozens of irrelevancies, compromises, and logrolling blocked action.

How serious this was appeared years later. I was invited back to the college to speak. Both members of the family with whom I was to stay were out, but I made my way to the familiar guest room. When my host returned I said, "I'll bet you were at an advisory committee meeting." "You win," he said. "Further," I said, "you were considering the case of Mr. X." "Right again," he replied. "And the decision," I concluded, "was that there was no tenure for him and he should seek a post elsewhere." "Correct once more, but how did you know?" "Simple," was my response, "that was the matter before the committee and its conclusion at the last meeting I attended before I resigned." Incidentally the man attained tenure and was promoted to a professorship by "adverse possession."

All too often what was said in the confidence of the committee was leaked abroad through inadvertence, forgetfulness—or deliberately, to block some unwelcome action when the man who broke confidence had been in a minority position. I became convinced that while advice was essential, it was sounder, more reliable, and vastly more confidential when it was not given in the presence of a group.

Once advice is institutionalized it loses much of its value.

The effect of experience on the advisory committee was to encourage me to take, privately, all the advice I could get, but keep the responsibility for decision in my own hands, thus avoiding the wifely complications and the log-rolling. I did not hold onto the determination of the issue because of faith in my superior wisdom; when the need is for decision, almost any competent and sincere individual is better than a committee.

One final phase in my training was making speeches, a necessary evil as all college presidents can testify. Like most elements in my career the beginning was accidental. The man who had been president during my freshman year was living in retirement in Middletown. He had agreed to speak to a local church group. On the day appointed he was taken ill and I was asked—ordered, really—to fill in. The several who had been approached earlier had all been able to avoid the assignment; my chief brooked no refusal. What my topic was, how it was developed I have long since forgotten. But the memory of the struggle to put something together in a single afternoon remains. At that time I was writing out all my classroom lectures, down to the last phrase. There was no time to do that, so I had to speak from notes, and I was terrified.

My second speech stands out with equal clarity. I was to lecture to the students in the divinity school downtown. Marsiglio of Padua was my subject—its relevance to their studies now seems to me peripheral in the extreme. My introduction was fantastic. On the way to the library where I was to speak the dean said: "You are a professor, aren't you?" "No," I replied, "an instructor." "You have your doctor's degree, I presume?" "No, my thesis is still to be done." When we reached the classroom, on that much acquaintance, I was given one of the most glowing introductions of my career—after a word of prayer! A few years ago I came across that lecture among my papers and was impressed with how much learning one can acquire in youth and how it can evaporate through the years.

After such a rugged beginning, speaking has ever remained an arduous matter. During the eleven years of my teaching I must have delivered between a hundred and fifty and two hundred speeches. In retrospect, in the light of subsequent pressures, the number does not seem impressive. Then I recall that in those same eleven years I taught ten different courses, each from scratch. All this was essential preparation for a college presidency.

My apprenticeship had one gap of major proportions. I had no experience whatever in college finance. I had never seen a budget, and doubt that there was anything like a formal instrument of that kind at Wesleyan. I had never had to read a balance sheet or make any analysis of a fiscal kind. There was, indeed, a pamphlet giving the checkered history of the University's endowment. That I had read with care, and mounting disgust. It showed how pious and upright men could dissipate "permanent" assets without intending to do so. The story left a deep impress on my mind, and I could never take lightly the nature of the fiduciary trust. But how to manage it was a closed book.

In the many years since this apprenticeship I have heard endless discussions of career planning and its vital importance. When the speaker is proclaiming his gospel it sounds logical and in some ways appealing. But here I have set down the development of my own career. At nearly every critical point its direction was determined by accident—by events beyond my control. A whole series of unconnected and uncontrolled events first stirred my ambition. My administrative experience grew out of war, ineligibility for military service, and the poverty of the college. Fund raising came from the accident of having written a book about war funds. And so on. Step by step one accident after another shaped my course.

There was no inconsistency involved. My commitment to teaching and research was deep. That induced me to decline lucrative offers for non-college work. Around that central string crystallized my career; to that extent it was planned. Yet in the event both teaching and research had to give way before administrative preoccupations—and they were radically different from those envisioned by a college junior impressed with the academic pageantry of a president's inauguration.

II

The Trustees

WHEN I assumed office at Lawrence, I had already had a good many experiences with trustees, had seen them meet their obligations—and also default upon them. For the next thirty years, however, they were to be a constant source of study and concern, in order to have them as effective a force as possible in the service of their institution.

Soon after I went to Brown someone asked me to state explicitly what I wanted from a trustee. My response was "work, wealth, and wisdom, preferably all three, but at least two of the three." That was candid enough, but rather less brutal than another terse summary attributed to a Midwest official: "give, get, or get out." The latter has a sound core, since general experience shows that from a third to a half of the gifts to an institution for major projects must come from the members of the governing board, either directly or through their efforts. Nevertheless, admitting the relevance of the aphorism, I consider it too narrow; it concentrates too heavily upon new resources. The preservation and expansion of old assets are just as important, and sometimes more difficult; they require hard, unremitting, undramatic work and wisdom, and do not provide the thrill that comes from acquiring a new building or new endowment for scholarships or a professorship.

The American college board of trustees is, so far as I know, a unique institution. It holds title to the college; its power is supreme in most matters, including the educational program. By law it has sweeping authority. Universities in Britain and on the Continent do not have such officers. Indeed, scholars from abroad have difficulty in understanding why there should be any such body. A good many members of American faculties also doubt its value and wish for the kind of university government that is common in Great Britain. Control of a professional organization by a lay group is often denounced as an anomaly. Yet, when the whole problem is faced with candor, no substitute has been found. It can be shown that there have been, during more than three centuries of educational history, many unwise, and even tyrannical, acts. On the other hand, under no alternative system have colleges adapted themselves so completely to the society they serve, multiplied so rapidly, grown so swiftly in student attendance, in buildings, libraries, laboratories, and endowments.

Speaking of trustees as an institution may well give a wrong impression of uniformity. Any such inference would be wholly misleading. The size of the trustee body, the range of its powers, the nature of its action, and the extent of its influence are determined in large measure by the terms of the charter of each specific college or university—and often by custom even more.

Both these sources of power and influence open the way for marked differences among institutions. Some boards are very small, as few as five or seven; others are very large, fifty or more. It takes no great effort of the imagination to see why groups so disparate in size will follow different procedures and function in sharply contrasting ways. For example, the small group may have no standing committees, or very few. The large board cannot operate without committees. Indeed, the reality may be that the duties of the trustees are partitioned among the committees and the whole body virtually rubber-stamps their conclusions.

The size of the board tends to determine the frequency of meeting; the working rule is that small boards meet often, large boards seldom. The smallest board with which I have any familiarity meets every two weeks; the largest only twice a year. Almost inevitably the whole board of trustees that meets but once or twice a year exercises a minimum of influence upon the details of administration; when meetings are frequent a small group can have a more intimate knowledge of what is happening from day to day and is likely to influence it more directly.

Most governing bodies are unicameral, but Brown, Bowdoin, and Harvard, for example, have two boards. There the similarities end. The functions assigned the two boards are not uniform in the several institutions; their procedures vary, as does their significance. But if the charters of institutions make widely different provisions, custom often has an even greater influence.

The Brown charter, for example, provides that each trustee and fellow shall "take the engagement of allegiance prescribed by the law of this colony to His Majesty King George the Third, his heirs and rightful successors to the crown of Great Britain." As Rhode Island, upon becoming independent, did not draw up a new constitution, but for well over half a century continued to use the colonial charter, so Brown never asked for a change in its charter in this respect, though a committee recommended such action. Inasmuch as the laws of the state required no allegiance to the king, the Brown corporation merely voted that the "engagement" should promise "true allegiance to bear to the

United States of America," and let the charter stand unaltered.

The charter of Brown also declares, in strong language, that "the instruction and immediate government of the College shall forever be and rest in the President and Fellows, or Fellowship." They are called a "learned faculty" and are empowered "to make, enact, and publish all such laws, statutes, regulations and ordinances . . . as shall seem to them meet for the successful instruction and government of said College." It is required that the Fellows and Trustees shall "at all times sit and act by separate and distinct powers" and the enactments of the Fellows are to be "laid before the Trustees, and with their approbation shall be of force and validity, but not otherwise." Clearly these provisions opened the road for the President and Fellows at Brown to exercise much the same sort of leadership and control as that of the President and Fellows of Harvard. Yet that did not happen. Custom, not the charter, produced a wholly different kind of government.

The trustees and fellows do indeed obey the charter; they "sit" separately—but in the same room at the same time with only an aisle between. They have two presiding officers, one secretary, and a common agenda. They also act separately. When a motion is made on one side it must be seconded on that side. It is then debated on both, the fellows meticulously addressing the president and the trustees the chancellor. The motion must be put on the side where it originated; when passed there the other body concurs or refuses to do so. Without concurrence nothing happens.

After my first meeting I asked Chief Justice Charles Evans Hughes, then a senior fellow, how any serious business could be accomplished with so extraordinarily complicated a procedure. He smiled and replied cryptically, "You will learn." He was right; though action required concurrence by both boards, and though we faced many difficult—and controversial—questions, there was a divided vote between the two bodies just once in the eighteen and a half years I was at Brown. It was over a minor issue—the use of modern or Georgian architecture for a proposed building. I wanted modern and the fellows, the "senior" body in age as well as rank, supported that recommendation; the trustees, who averaged at least ten years younger, voted for Georgian. Thus my recommendation failed and the Georgian style remained by reason of a prior vote.

Experience with so unique—not to say clumsy—a system shows how almost any corporate structure can be made to operate where good will and good sense are dominant. For example, the Brown charter takes no account of the existence of a faculty, much less does it grant any powers to that body, although it actually exercises all the functions common to faculties elsewhere. There is, indeed, provision for the election of professors, and a hint, in a subordinate clause, that professors might also be fellows. There were instances of such service at an early time, but there have been none for more than a century. In 1844 the corporation voted that no professor should hold a seat in either the fellows or trustees.

Presumably every appointment to the faculty would require approval of the fellows, as do all changes in the curriculum even now. In practice, however, appointments are voted by the Advisory and Executive Committee (technically the "minor quorum" of the corporation which consists of at least four trustees and three fellows) and approved *ex post facto*, en masse, by the corporation at its semiannual meetings, without comment or discussion. In a set of minutes lying before me there are seventeen solid, single-spaced pages of retirements, resignations, appointments, designations, and all the other acts common to large and complicated organizations of personnel. The whole body of such matters was dealt with in a single omnibus vote which covered no less than fifty-one other, and separate, items.

The fellows vote all degrees, but, save for honorary degrees, do so only on recommendation of the faculty and, in modern times, without any deviation from that recommendation. In fact, under present conditions any failure to follow the faculty recommendation is virtually unthinkable. Time and custom have transferred the substance of power to the faculty, leaving the fellows only its formal exercise. Honorary degrees remain the sole prerogative of the fellows—sometimes exercised with advice, and at other times as quixotically as could possibly be imagined.

By charter all trustees and fellows are elected for life. The strict letter of the law is followed so far as fellows are concerned. Indeed, it has been sardonically asserted by critics that election to the fellowship is a virtual guaranty of longevity. However, all trustees agree to resign at the end of a seven-year term. Provisions about possible reelection have varied from time to time. Also some trustees are "nominated" by the alumni and the nomination is equivalent to election. All this is governed by custom, usually embodied in votes, which of course would not be binding against the charter, if challenged. Custom has altered the substance, though not the word or the final authority, of the charter.

In short, the institution referred to by the generic term of board of trustees involves an almost infinite variety of composition, powers, procedures, and influence. Not only do charters provide great variability, custom adds other variants. When one speaks of the functions of boards of trustees in American colleges or universities the generalizations are all subject to practically innumerable exceptions.

In line with that remark, there have been developments through custom which have been no less than revolutionary.

Academic freedom was a concept unknown to the early colleges and universities. Professors and presidents were dismissed for religious beliefs, for scientific views, for political positions, or for any of a wide range of actions or words that displeased the omnipotent trustees. Such episodes, though still not unknown, have become increasingly rare in recent years. The damage suffered by an institution when its governing board trespasses upon academic freedom has become so severe that trustees exhibit more and more restraint in the exercise of their charter authority.

The first, and in many ways the most important, duty of the trustees is to elect the president. Unfortunately it is a function for which the board has only the meagerest competence. This deficiency is not personal; it stems from a number of circumstances.

To begin with, if the institution has been well managed and fortunate, the trustees who must perform the function have had no experience in the matter. All, or nearly all, the men and women who chose the last president would be out of office. The new group, never having done it before, are not well equipped for this, their most vital task.

The second difficulty arises when they ask themselves what kind of man should be chosen. Boards are tempted to write a list of specifications. When everyone has had his say, no one less than the Archangel Gabriel could meet the bill of particulars—and he is not available. Instead of revising the qualifications realistically, the trustees persist in seeking the perfect man. This often has a disastrous effect. The selection committee starts enthusiastically and is impressed with the number of suggestions which flow in to it. Time passes, the winnowing proceeds, yet the flawless candidate fails to appear. Then fatigue settles in, and when it grows acute, as it often does, the committee is likely to choose someone who is "available." The choice is all too often a person of less talent and character than others who were passed over while the members still had stars in their eyes.

I have seen many such instances. One episode stands out in my memory. A board of trustees had given too much authority to a president and had trusted him too implicitly. On his death it was clear that the institution was in serious financial trouble. Search for a president was pursued for several weeks without success. Someone advised the committee to consult with me. The chairman, a man of great vigor and strength of will, did so, over the telephone. I was familiar with the circumstances and said, without much finesse, that they had to make a choice—they could have a "name" but only an administrator past his prime and not able to do the hard, grinding work necessary to put the institution in good shape again, or they could take an unknown whose name would add no prestige, but whose energies and skill might save the situation. Rather abruptly the chairman said the dilemma was not that sharp—and hung up. My feelings were not injured. My advice had been worth all it cost, since there was no compensation involved.

Two weeks later the phone rang; it was the chairman. With no preliminaries he blurted, "You were right; who is the unknown." I mentioned a name; he was elected within a week and took office within ten days. The trustees, having once given a president too much power, sought to compensate by putting in a business manager without the approval of the new president. They reckoned without their host. He made the matter one of confidence, and said he would resign at once—on his second or third day of office—if the appointment was made. So drastic a crisis the trustees could not face. He won not only that round, but every succeeding one, and proved just the man for the tough job of restoring solvency and standards. In that instance, a rare one, fatigue in the search ultimately led to a realistic estimate of the situation and a wise choice.

Most lists of candidates are too long. Again and again one reads in the paper, when a new president is elected, that he was chosen as the best among a hundred, two hundred, or more persons "considered." This is sheer nonsense. The chapter in *Parkinson's Law* entitled "The Short List" should be required reading for all committees seeking a president. With satiric wit the author presents the "principles upon which the choice" among candidates should be made. Using the British civil service as the basis, he discusses the problem and concludes that "the Chinese method" is best; it consists of throwing all the applications into the waste basket, considering only one candidate, "and he a man who did not apply." Parkinson asserts "that the failure of other methods is mainly due to there being too many candidates." There is much wisdom amid the satire. Persons who apply for the office of president should always—practically always—be neglected. This is one job which should seek the man.

A second sound principle is involved: the list that is too long has been carelessly drawn; it reflects confusion. No committee can make any worth-while, perceptive investigation of hundreds of persons. Inevitably, when confronted with so many names, a good many are dropped on superficial grounds. One of the most conspicuous presidents in the country was eliminated from consideration that way. His name was later restored to "consideration" almost by accident.

The problem of choosing the right man for a presidency is made more difficult because there is now no obvious place to look. No standard progression from one post to another leads to the college presidency. Up to fifty years ago most presidents were clergymen. All my predecessors at Lawrence had been Methodist ministers; all my predecessors at Brown were Baptist preachers. That was natural; most colleges were founded upon a religious impulse and had strong church connections. Early curriculums reflected this interest. Moreover, for long years the clergy was the only learned profession. Ministers were scholars of a sort—or supposed to be. They were "interested in youth"; they were accustomed to working with boards of control under a wide variety of names. They had practice in making a dollar go further than was reasonable; they had experience raising money. Almost all could speak, and "a few words of inspiration" were called for—and still are—more often than any other type of speech.

As long as the majority of colleges were church-related there was a denominational guide to selection. It was relatively easy to hear a preacher, talk with members of his parish, and find out a great deal about him. Once secularism became dominant, the eyes of the trustees turned elsewhere. What guide was possible?

Most trustees are businessmen; naturally they want a businesslike administration. As a consequence they have sometimes selected men with financial skill—such as Thomas Sovereign Gates, who was President of the University of Pennsylvania for nearly fifteen years. He had been a Morgan partner. Such a man gives up a lucrative position to accept a university presidency as a public service. It is not difficult for businessmen as trustees to make such a choice if their candidate is willing; they know his qualities. What they cannot always judge is his adaptability to the peculiarities of university management, with its extraordinary differences from business.

Obviously in making such a choice they are either aware of those differences, and expect the president to delegate many of his academic responsibilities, or they are unclear in their estimate of a president's duties. Fifty years ago Charles William Eliot stressed the difference between business and education and remarked that "many of the things" a trustee "has learnt to value in his business experience he will have to discard absolutely in contributing to the management of a university, for they are inapplicable." That is still sound doctrine. The Columbia University report on *The Role of the Trustees* puts it succinctly: "businessmen must do everything they can to make certain that they do not carry over from business life any customs, procedures, or attitudes of mind which, no matter how appropriate to business, do not belong in the university atmosphere—and not only do not belong but can do it harm." Not always, by any means, but often the election of a businessman to the presidency of a college reflects the failure of the trustees to recognize this truth.

A third group of university and college presidents have been drawn from the military. An early and famous instance was the election of Robert E. Lee to head Washington College (now Washington and Lee University) after the Civil War. Generals Mark W. Clark, Andrew D. Bruce, and Dwight D. Eisenhower and Admiral Richard L. Conolly are recent illustrations. These choices are often—if not always—"prestige" elections; they are designed to reflect the importance of the institution through the person of a man who has already had a career of great distinction.

Such officers also have the advantage of training in managing a complex organization, delegating authority while retaining and exercising responsible control. Generals and admirals have the kind of all-round experience most university presidents need. They have had contact, earlier in their careers, with young men of college age; they know the problems of discipline. Most of them have spent from a third to half their periods of active service in schools of a professional character. In addition they can be readily identified; their characteristics are well known. They are not likely to develop traits that could not have been foreseen by those who chose them—if their inquiries have been more than perfunctory. However, academic freedom is one phase of university life that is alien to their earlier experience and relationship to the faculty may prove troublesome.

A fourth source of college presidents is public officials. Former Governor Horace A. Hildreth of Maine went to Bucknell, and former Governor Harold E. Stassen to the University of Pennsylvania, for example. Such choices are also "prestige" appointments, and are relatively easy to make. There is no difficulty in finding out about the man, his speaking ability, his deftness in dealing with personnel problems, his gift for public relations, his administrative capacity. The weakness of such appointments is that usually they do not represent any profound commitment on the part of the appointee; they are apt to be transient or at least transitory. When, and if, something "better" comes along the trustees may be faced with doing their work all over again.

Another type of choice that is relatively easy for a board of trustees is one of their own number. That was the case when Mr. Gates was selected as President of the University of Pennsylvania. He had been an active alumnus, interested in fund raising, a trustee of the University and chairman of the executive committee of the board. Ethan A. H. Shepley, now Chancellor of Washington University, St. Louis, was a long-time member of its board, and chairman at the time of his election. Such instances are not uncommon, and they seldom bring surprises. The men are well known to their colleagues, they are familiar with many phases of the university's problems, they make a sacrifice in accepting the post and a deep commitment from which they are unlikely to withdraw.

Another obvious place to search is among the alumni.

Graduates who merit consideration are reasonably easy to identify; their records, if they have been "good" alumni, are available. Their friends and associates can be interviewed discreetly. But there is a very large fly in the ointment. Selection of a president should never be a sentimental matter. In my experience no other group, when surveyed, leads to so many suggestions based on sentiment—and sentiment alone. Often people seem to think of the presidency as some kind of medal or reward, not as a task calling for special qualifications and the fullest exertion of all a man's powers.

College business officers form another group to which trustees sometimes turn. And there is a good deal of logic in such a move. During the last thirty-five years the business management of colleges has become a recognized profession. Since from the point of view of most trustees the visible problems are chiefly financial, it is a natural inference that a business officer would make a good president. The most conspicuous illustration is Robert Gordon Sproul. He served as Comptroller of the University of California for a decade before he became president in 1930. The University of Illinois chose Lloyd Morey, long its business manager, as president for a brief term.

However logical the choice, the fact remains that faculties tend to resist—directly or indirectly—the appointment of business officers. They are apt to look upon the chief fiscal officer as essentially a "no" man; they normally expect him to put fiscal considerations ahead of better teaching and research. Sometimes these impressions are valid, more often they are not. But of the reality of the prejudice there can be no doubt. Except for that fact there would be many more such choices.

The last source—now the largest, the most important, and the most difficult from which to make a choice—is composed of scholars. Selection of a scholar is difficult because trustees are not well acquainted with the world of scholarship and ordinarily have very inadequate means of investigation. Indeed, they seldom know how to evaluate what they are able to find out, for scholarship accentuates a whole set of values with which most trustees have had only the most casual contact. Such choices present difficulties, also, because there is no sure way to tell how a teacher and research man will behave administratively, how he will develop in the radically different environment in which he will thenceforth move. Of course, if a man has been a dean and has shown managerial skill, has learned to expound policy to the alumni and the public, he is likely to be deluged with opportunities. And larger institutions often choose presidents of smaller institutions. But once these two sources are exhausted the task of discovery and selection of a scholar becomes extremely difficult.

The consequence is that often the same post will be offered in succession to men whose educational philosophies and methods are radically different; yet the trustee committee seems blissfully unaware of that fact, though it deems definite qualifications to be central to its choice. In one instance, with which I was intimately familiar, the presidency was offered to a university dean who appeared on every list of prospects for some years. He was a noted follower of the one-stop-service-station concept of a college; there was no secret about his views since he was highly articulate. If he had accepted the office he would have filled the curriculum with "practical" courses. For various reasons he declined the invitation. The trustees next offered the post to a scholar who had no administrative experience whatever and had shown not the slightest interest in it. He was an advocate of the liberal arts of the purest kind. He accepted.

Incidentally, the first man later accepted a university presidency and then resigned in disillusionment after two years;

the scholar who was such an administrative gamble performed brilliantly and went on ultimately to one of the most distinguished educational positions in the world. Both these men were "scholars" in the technical sense, but that omnibus word concealed differences so radical that the college would have followed policies the exact reverse of its tradition if the committee's original choice had accepted.

Indeed, I can speak from personal experience. Within a span of a few years I was offered a series of supposed "promotions." One was to a great state university with a tradition of acute instability in its executive leadership. I have been acquainted with eight of its presidents. It was a post for which I had neither taste nor qualification; it involved working with a state legislature that liked to interfere; it required compromises and political deftness which were outside my nature. When I declined promptly and firmly, the regents chose a man whose views, methods, and temperament contrasted sharply with mine.

Soon afterward I was urged so hard to head another state university that I finally visited the institution, and saw at once that it did not suit my book—and that I was not what was needed for its program. When I resisted great pressure and declined, the presidency was next offered to a man whose administrative policy was as near 180 degrees from mine as could be measured—and he was well adapted to the position. In neither case, so far as I could see, did the governing boards appreciate that they were not only choosing a man but also determining basic educational policies at the same time.

The clearest proof that this, the first and most important, task of trustees is not well performed is to be found in the shortness of tenure in office of college presidents. The average is said to be about four years. As I reflect upon the short administrations I have known, the reasons for their brevity should, in almost every instance, have been clear before the appointment. A politician elected a college president resigned to take an ambassador's post. An institution with a strongly conservative clerical group on its board chose a man whose religious views were extremely liberal and who regularly drank and served cocktails. A "business" group that dominated one board became discontented because the new president sought to discontinue undergraduate business administration courses which he felt bordered on fraud.

In another instance the trustees chose a man who had been dismissed from a deanship and was both arrogant and sycophantic in his next post—qualities that should have made him ineligible if any reasonable investigation had been made. As a "blueprint" he had all the right lines—a doctor of philosophy degree from a great university, administrative experience in two good colleges. As a man he was not reliable—as three successive institutions found to their sorrow. A state university president offended politicians by insisting upon academic standards and was "let out." A preacher took a presidency of a college expecting a three months' vacation on his farm—only to be rudely told to come back because he was entitled to a couple of weeks. He resigned to accept the headmastership of a school near his farm! And so goes the list. From my own acquaintance it could be indefinitely extended. In every case of a short administration I can recall, a reasonably competent investigation beforehand would have made such misfit appointments much less likely.

Short administrations are a great loss because institutional momentum is seriously impaired. But there is another bad result of poor choices; this occurs when the trustees, having elected the wrong man, lack either the courage or the skill to remove him from office. He, on his part, has often burned his bridges behind him. He realizes that there are few worse drugs on the market than an ex-college president; so he clings to the position beyond the period of his usefulness because he does not have access to an acceptable alternative. What I had not realized in my Wesleyan days was how common is trustee discontent with a president, and how often an unsatisfactory situation runs on several years for lack of knowledge as to how to act with both resolution and justice.

The relevance of these comments about trustees in a discussion of the college presidency should be obvious, for in filling this office the board is exercising its highest responsibility. In nine cases out of ten, however, the choice is not made in reality by the board, but by a small committee thereof. Usually one or two persons on that committee do all or most of the work. The rest of the committee and the board as a whole accept the recommendation in the faith that the one or two have done their work well.

As I write these words I am acutely conscious of the fact that it is relatively easy to show how to avoid poor or inappropriate appointments, but infinitely more difficult to explain how to make good ones. Some suggestions are implicit in what has already been said. The committee on selection should be composed of people in whom the board has deep confidence; it is no casual assignment to be made in an offhand manner. Those who accept appointment must be ready to give time and thought to the work, and not try to fob it off on the chairman and one or two others. The decisions are sufficiently important to have the substance of collective judgment, not just the form.

The bill of specifications should not be an exercise in either wishful thinking or defeatist assumptions; it should rest on analysis of the needs of the institution over the next decade, so far as they can be foreseen. It should not be too dogmatic about the age of the new appointee. After a long tenure—perhaps a shade too long—there is a tendency to overaccentuate "youth." After experience with a "young" man with more brashness than wisdom, trustees yearn for "maturity." The office should be open to young men of brilliant promise, and to older men who have proved themselves and may be able to serve only ten years or so.

Above all the appointee should be chosen for his talents, not for his reputation. I recall vividly a long telephone conversation with a chairman of a selection committee; he had a man in mind, but that man was "unknown." My response was to express a point of view which has grown stronger through the years: "Pay no attention to that supposed deficiency. The institution has great prestige. You can afford to lend him some of that for a time; the fact that you choose him will make him known fast enough. If he is as good as you think he is, he will repay the loan many fold." He was elected and fulfilled my prediction. The fact is that a man's reputation is seldom, or never, up-to-date. Either he has earned recognition not yet accorded him, or he is living on a reputation earned in the past but no longer being built up.

The selection committee will do better to study the qualifications of a few men and women intensively instead of confusing their minds with a vast number. In studying qualifications they should seek advice. Officials of the great philanthropic foundations know where the live wires are; they can identify men who give unusual promise, for such men are normally among those seeking grants. The committee can turn to college and university presidents for suggestions. The members can get help from faculties. This offers some difficulties. Sometimes a faculty committee can be of assistance; more often, perhaps, it tends to confuse issues.

To my mind the best method is to identify some good

intermediary who has access to faculty opinion. In one instance that came under my observation the selection committee was enthusiastic about a scientist with a wide reputation. The institution seeking a president had a strong department in his field. The intermediary casually inquired of the chairman of the department how its members would look upon the candidate as a colleague. The reaction was negative —vigorously. It was suggested that he might seek the views of his associates. With one consent they were in opposition and the name was dropped. This did not mean that the man was unfit; it meant he did not fit that particular post.

It is not possible to lay down a set of rules that will guarantee success. There is always some gamble involved. Even when trustees have exerted their best efforts, and with reasonable skill, they may be surprised. John Hay made a sardonic comment on marriage: "Why should you worry in choosing whom you should marry? Choose whom you may, you will find you have got somebody else." If courtship reveals so little as to justify any such remark in even the slightest degree, how much more true is it that the new college president may turn out to be a quite different man from the one the trustees thought they were electing. Sometimes, as in marriage, the "somebody else" is better than anticipated, by far. At other times the denouement is not so happy. In any event, there will be surprises.

When I reached Lawrence this certainly proved to be the case. A leading trustee reminded me of my "youth" and inexperience; he suggested that each Saturday evening I should come to his home, there to meet with a small group to "lay out the next week's work." He said that my predecessor—who had been master of his job if any college president ever was—had followed that procedure. If he pursued any such routine, I am confident that he and no one else did the "laying out."

Here, at the very outset, I found that supervision by the trustees, which every charter provides either explicitly or by inference, was to be taken over by a single dominant figure. Moreover, such supervision was not to consist in approving general policies, leaving to the president the means and methods of carrying them out. Instead it was to be a detailed, explicit, review of day-to-day events with the purpose of shaping specific action.

In retrospect I see no reason to doubt that the proposal was well intentioned. The trustee had been a faculty member at one time, he had lively intellectual interests, he was one of the largest, if not the largest donor to the college. He knew its faculty and its traditions intimately. Moreover, I realized that I needed counsel. But I did not want a cicerone, and declined the invitation. Subsequently I learned that had I followed the suggested routine it would have seriously impaired my ability to work with other trustees. There are almost always crosscurrents within any large board. If the president ties himself too closely to one group, he may get into serious trouble with another. He must pretend as long as possible that there are no factions and bend his energies to bringing all the trustees together so that factionalism is ended.

The situation at Lawrence was more difficult because, as I speedily discovered, most trustees had only the vaguest knowledge of the business of the college. My predecessor had been in office thirty years, and by reason of experience, ability, and tact he had dominated the board as well as every phase of daily operation. The chairman of the trustees lived at a distance and was not on the executive committee, nor were his relations with some members of that group all that could be desired. The chairman of the executive committee was elderly and not active between sessions. The chairman of the investment committee and the treasurer were very close and tended to dominate the rest. In short, I found out what many another president has learned after he took office: "the board of trustees" was, to most intents and purposes, a very small clique. What it determined the board accepted, and without much review or discussion.

It was soon evident that if I was to be effective I must do one of two things: join the clique or beat it. Why not join it? I could not, because it was following policies which I could not approve. This struck me with great force at the end of the first fiscal year of my term of office. Because I was totally inexperienced, the treasurer (a man not very successful in his own business) and the business manager (a professor of business in whom I quickly lost confidence) really controlled fiscal matters. The interim reports I received during the year were usually verbal, and to call them sketchy is to make them sound more substantial than they were. When time came to close the books a conference was called in my office.

The question posed by the treasurer was explicit: "How much deficit do you want to show?" I was thunderstruck. "What," I asked, "is the difference between income and expenditure?" The answer was "about $50,000." "That," I said, "is the deficit." "Oh, no," was the instant rejoinder, "the trustees would not like it"! I said, "Close the books as you please this year," determined never again to be put in such a position. The deficit was "made" a modest amount in appearance by "capitalizing" books bought for the library and several other expenditures which I regarded as current expense. That meant, as I saw it, misappropriating endowment funds.

Two things I did promptly: I learned, with the active and patient help of another trustee, to read a balance sheet; and I studied the principles of college accounting with fiery zeal. I relieved the business manager of his post—and shortly of his professorship—and sought a new one. There ensued a tussle with the "insiders." The position seemed to them an ideal one to "take care of" a man who had headed a small bank that failed. I was forced to consult him, but made the work sound at least as difficult as I knew it was. He helped me immensely by declining to accept large fiscal responsibility again; he preferred a clerkship. Because the clique could produce no other candidate I sought and, with the help of Horace Ford of the Massachusetts Institute of Technology, found a skilled professional who worked intimately with me as long as I was at Lawrence and continued to serve under two of my successors. Ultimately I was able to get the head of the largest bank in the state to serve as treasurer; this "prestige" appointment could not be resisted by any member of the board. The effect was to give me and the business manager full control of day-to-day operations.

Breaking the grip of the small inside group who controlled investment policy was more difficult. Even before my arrival, when I was being interviewed, I expressed some skepticism that endowment could bring such a high rate of interest as the income indicated. The chairman of the investment committee told me that opinion was a consequence of my New England experience, that Midwestern rates were higher. I had no basis upon which to argue the point. But as I began to learn about fiscal matters I was more and more disturbed. Changes in endowment investments seemed to be made with a high degree of informality. In effect one man controlled the whole process, and the record was not explicit or precise.

At last there was a substitution of one set of securities for another that seemed to me definitely to downgrade a sizable investment. I was not on the investment committee even *ex officio;* nevertheless, the matter seemed so important that I lodged a protest with the chairman. His answer was that he had given the first set of securities and felt he had the right to substitute others from time to time as his judgment dictated. I remarked that the change did not seem to be determined by the interests of the college, but had the effect of strengthening his own credit position. Without hesitation he agreed that was the case, but pointed out that if he was to continue to give substantial amounts he must have a good deal to say about the management of the funds he had given. I made it clear that as a matter of principle I would resist any such practice. His response was explicit: "I do not think you can succeed, but if you do I shall take my benefactions elsewhere."

I was licked. No other word is adequate. The committee was in his pocket, and the board of trustees was in the dark. Events played into my hands; within a year the substituted securities defaulted, and I called for new securities, which were finally conceded. There were three results: first, the loss of a thoroughly interested, generous trustee, whose concern for the college was deep and genuine, but whose methods seemed to me improper. The second result was happier—the establishment of a new investment committee which has functioned ever since with great devotion and success. The third lesson I learned was that the president must be *ex officio* on all trustee committees—and work on them. Both at Lawrence and at Brown I attended the investment committee meetings every possible time and followed the work closely.

One other bitter battle had to be fought before the office of president had any significant meaning. Student discipline, by terms of the charter, was in the hands of the president and faculty. It seemed to me that the responsibility was not well discharged. Standards were unclear and quixotically administered. More particularly, cheating was rampant and virtually unchecked. I had grown up under the honor system and in my student days had never seen anyone cheat; the only students whom others saw were promptly punished by student action. During my years of teaching I had watched the students police the honesty of examinations with courage and success. I found that an honor system was impossible in Wisconsin not because the students were less honest, but because the regional tradition was hostile. So I made it clear that anyone caught cheating would be sent home.

Suddenly two boys, both of prominent families in a neighboring state, were discovered to have turned in papers copied word for word from an encyclopedia. The evidence was clear, and without more ado I sent the boys home. One of them was a roommate of the son of a member of the executive committee. At its next meeting the man challenged the wisdom of my action. I called the attention of the committee to the charter provisions, but they insisted that they would nonetheless review the matter. Thereupon I announced I was out of office, left the meeting, and went home. It was some two hours before an emissary came to say that if I would return the trustees would not again interfere with discipline. My relations with that particular member of the committee thereafter were excellent.

Nevertheless, the episode confirmed an opinion which had been maturing for some time. The position of the president is essentially political; that is, it is only so strong at any given time as his standing with his trustees. He must be ready to demand, directly or by inference, a vote of confidence when his authority is challenged in any serious way. Moreover, he must be ready to give up his office if confidence is lacking. When the president dare not resign, his powers are waning and soon he will be impotent. Never again did I have to force a showdown in such explicit terms, but, when the going was rocky or the situation tense, I chose a board member upon whose discretion and judgment I could rely and had him, ostensibly on his own initiative, take an informal poll among his fellow members. Many a trustee who will not face the president with his discontents will reveal them to another member of the board. Keeping his fences mended with his trustees is a vital matter for a president who wants to do something besides merely cling to office.

The same incident—the dismissal of two cheats—highlighted a lesson I had learned very early in my teaching years: a trustee is entitled to no special consideration in matters of principle by reason of his office. In one of my classes was the son of a wealthy trustee. He did poor work and I failed him; but the professor in the department (there was just one) was unwilling to countersign the grade until I "explained" it to the president. So I went to the front office and started to tell the story. He interrupted me with his characteristic "Hennery": "You are here to teach. If we think you are not competent we will dismiss you, but as long as you teach your grades are none of my business. Moreover, the son of a trustee is just another student and his parentage is no concern of yours." The denouement was dramatic. The trustee resigned, deleted a bequest of half a million for the college, and died within six months. When I was on more familiar terms with the president I asked him if he remembered the case. "How could I forget it? Nevertheless, it was the only thing to do." After so striking a lesson no trustee's son could ever expect preferential treatment, much less his roommate!

Aside from my inexperience, many of my difficulties arose from a single source. Members of the board of trustees, in general, were not in close enough touch to deal effectively with the problems of the college. The board was large; its members were scattered; it met only twice a year; it had few active committees. The powers of the board fell, by default, into the hands of an active, interested group who sought to move from supervision to management until there seemed to me to be clear trespass upon the duties of the president.

I have seen it happen again and again. In one dramatic instance in connection with the North Central Association of Colleges and Secondary Schools I learned a bitter lesson. A university was before the Board of Review (the policing authority) in the process of losing its accreditation. The newly elected president was an amiable man near retirement age; in fact, it seemed he had been chosen because he was known to be pliable. Policy was determined by the chairman of the trustees and his son who had been made treasurer (with the powers of business manager as well). They had their offices downtown, miles from the university. They had induced the board of trustees to adopt by-laws which conferred extraordinary powers upon them. In appearance, at least, they were treating the institution as a proprietary interest, were setting athletic and other policies, and exercising powers that belonged to the faculty. The president was simply a "front man" for their operations.

As consideration of the case approached the critical phase they resorted to pressure tactics. A former student of mine was editor of the leading newspaper in the city. He was flown to Chicago in a private plane to see me. I had liked him as a student; when he arrived, therefore, I listened to his arguments and his exposition of what would happen if accreditation were withdrawn. When he was through, I asked him what he thought I would do. He smiled and said, "I told them it was no use, that their tactics were wrong." With no further argument he flew home.

The next arrival was the chairman of the board of trustees in person. He was contrite, cooperative, protesting he meant no wrong and had drawn the by-laws in good faith but in ignorance of acceptable practice. The Board of Review took him at his word; a group, of whom I was simple enough to be one, sat up all night drafting new by-laws. Accreditation was "saved"—but soon the old practices were revived; the loudly proclaimed "good faith" was missing. The results were what might have been expected. The president retired, and the board elected a vigorous, but rash, man who soon clashed with the leading trustees; a damaging row ensued which injured the university still more. The episode recalled the acid comment, a century before, of Thomas Arnold, the famous headmaster of Rugby: "No man ought to meddle with universities who does not know them well and love them well."

All these episodes—and dozens more could be added—make it clear that the first duty of a president is to try to inform all his trustees, interest as many of them as he can, and urge them to exercise their full powers. They should neither surrender them to a small "inside" group nor trespass upon the functions of faculty and administrative officers.

How simple that sounds! Yet it is one of the most complex problems a president has to face. If, in the effort to achieve this worthy end, he sends long and explicit reports, he may be well assured that they will not be read by most trustees. If he sends frequent short letters, the issues are not made clear. If he attempts personal visits, they must be managed with great skill to produce the desired effect. Moreover, the process must be continuous. For the personnel of a board changes far more rapidly than it appears to from the outside. New members need a good deal of indoctrination; it requires at least three years before a new trustee is familiar with procedures, problems, and policies. Very few can make a large contribution—other than financial—without at least that many years of careful cultivation.

Not only does the personnel of the board change; there is also constant—and occasionally swift—change in the problems to be faced. As one who administered a college through the Great Depression and a university through the Second World War I am acutely conscious of the basic issues that come up again and again. But I am equally aware of the new problems, kaleidoscopic in their complexity and rapidity of change in outlines and colors. Different times and altered circumstances require new policies; therefore, if a president is wise he will seek to keep his trustees alert and informed. In a remarkable passage, the committee emphasized this point in *The Role of the Trustees of Columbia University:* "it is the constant desire of the trustees to be instructed at the same time that they carry out their final responsibilities for the kind and quality of instruction provided." For that guidance, the president is directly responsible.

Sometimes even the simplest phase of this task proves unexpectedly difficult. It had long been the practice of the Advisory and Executive Committee at Brown not to send the minutes of its meetings to the other members of the corporation. There was nothing sinister about the reasons; apparently some executive actions, all of which required subsequent approval by the whole governing body, had been prematurely revealed, causing difficulties. When the corporation met every action was always fully and fairly reported, so no attempt at concealment was involved. But an enormous amount of detail was presented during each semiannual meeting; consequently the opportunity for questions and discussion was limited by time. The danger of embarrassment by premature disclosure seemed to me less a hazard than having the governing body uninformed for considerable periods. Moreover, the practice gave the appearance of concealment, even though that purpose was nonexistent.

After two or three years I succeeded in having the "executive actions"—a bare skeleton record—sent to all corporation members each month. Within another few years a full account not only of executive actions but of the president's informal report and the substance of the advisory discussion was circulated. To make the whole process even more informative, nonmembers of the committee were invited in rotation to attend meetings and participate. People who had regarded themselves as "outsiders" lost that sense of isolation. They also learned at first hand how seriously the committee took its work, and how freely my proposals were discussed and modified before being put to a vote.

The second duty of a president, in relation to his trustees, is to strengthen the personnel of his board. Usually boards are self-perpetuating. Customarily there is a committee to make suggestions for filling vacancies; it longs for guidance, even when it appears to resist it. Without dictating, a president can help to shape the board of trustees in a relatively few years. Indeed, one of the best tests of the quality of an administration is the kind of board in office when the president retires.

To manage matters wisely, he needs to have a pattern of what is already there—by age, by profession, by resources, by interest. He does not want a board all of one age; more particularly, he must be careful not to let the board grow old with him. There is an almost inevitable tendency to choose men and women of his own time—they are the ones for whom he feels some "natural affinity." That temptation must be firmly resisted. Moreover, he needs different kinds of men and women for different work: some for the finance committee, some for investments, some for faculty affairs.

By keeping a running inventory of the personnel of the board he knows where the most serious gaps in its structure are to be found. By seeking the best persons for specific tasks on the board he will prevent the committee from mistakenly nominating someone as a kind of "reward." Membership *is*, and ought to be, "recognition," but it is also, and much more, a task. One of the commonest and most serious mistakes is to take a man because he is a "good fellow" or "has represented us well." The test question is: Will he contribute work, wealth, and wisdom? Unless the answer is in the affirmative, he should be passed over, however amiable or popular.

It is extraordinary how slowly the position of women has been recognized in boards of trustees, particularly in the East. When I went to Lawrence College in 1925 there were four or five women on the board; one was chairman of the buildings and grounds committee—and a good one. Before many years a woman was appointed to the executive committee. Brown, despite the fact that Pembroke College had been part of the University for half a century, had never elected a woman. Yet women control much of the wealth of the nation; many are extremely good workers; in numerous fields their judgment is invaluable. Nevertheless, it required twelve years of patient effort before the first woman trustee was appointed. After that election further such nominations occasioned no resistance, indeed no remark. Soon a woman served on the Advisory and Executive Committee, and a woman member of the committee to nominate my successor played an unpublicized but important part. Tradition is stubborn, but brittle; once shattered it is no longer a barrier.

In offering suggestions the president should be as impersonal and analytical as possible. His fundamental relationship with the board should be one of mutual respect.

Friendships—and close ones—he will inevitably form, but friendship is a poor basis for the selection of trustees; it may make the administrative work temporarily easier, but it is certain to make it less stimulating and effective. Too close personal ties between the president and trustees may also result in troubles for his successor, for when retirement comes there will be reluctance to accept a new leader.

Of course the president cannot appoint his own governors—but if he does not influence their election the results are not likely to increase the strength of the board. And strength is what is needed beyond all else. I have already mentioned that one of the greatest contributions President Shanklin made at Wesleyan was in influencing strong men to join the board. Several came to disapprove of him, yet in the long run they gave the college fiscal independence and, under new leadership, treated the faculty with a respect all too rare in the college world.

In the search for good trustees a president is not wise to expect perfection. One of the best trustees at Lawrence, a man of sound judgment in nearly everything, harried me about the teaching of economics. He gave me the "as the twig is bent" routine until I was weary to the point of exhaustion. It did no good to assure him that instruction in the department was as competent as any in the college; talk of academic freedom made no impression whatever. When I told my troubles to one of his college contemporaries, he said, "Why at college he became a devotee of Henry George, and was a rabid single taxer." I made no comment but the next time the trustee came to warn me of the bent twigs, I remarked that he had been a single tax enthusiast in his youth, then asked, "What changed your mind?" Without a flicker of humor he responded, "I bought a piece of property." My only comment was a broad grin; he never complained of economic instruction again. The strengths of trustees must be used for the benefit of the college, their deficiencies shrugged off.

The president should be candid in dealing with the board. That does not involve exposing his feelings on every matter. In one tragic instance that I remember vividly the unwise expression of feeling made infinite trouble for everyone involved. Three men, all full professors with "tenure," two of them close to retirement, were indubitably poor teachers. One was a valuable member of the faculty; whatever his deficiencies in the classroom, he was splendid in counsel. He could demolish proposed academic folly with deadly effect; sometimes, unhappily for him, it was one of the president's proposals. The second professor had, so far as I could discover, no worth in the classroom, in committee, or in the faculty. He had "scholarship" in a highly dessicated form; it was precise, impeccable, and vastly dull. He had some money. The third was possessed of no skill as teacher, scholar, or counselor—and had no money. He had been appointed when the post was under such a cloud that no good man would accept it.

Many of their colleagues found their established positions in the academic hierarchy irksome, yet were willing to accept the situation lest academic freedom be imperiled. Actually there were measures which could have been taken if there had been resourcefulness and courage available in the right quarters and in adequate quantities.

In any event, the president, impatient and frustrated, conveyed his annoyance to the trustees. Thereupon a proposal was made to omit the three names from the list when the faculty was given a general increase in salary. Professors who felt that the adverse discrimination was to a large extent justified nonetheless believed that the principle was dangerous; if the president and trustees could show fiscal favoritism, they could punish independence, interpreted as "disloyalty."

The president, by expressing himself with too much irritation to the trustees, had managed to kick up a storm over academic privilege and security. The episode ended disgracefully. The professor with money said his will provided that all his estate should go to the college; if he were discriminated against, he would alter his will. Promptly, the three were given advances in salary with the rest. It was the worst case of "money talks" I ever witnessed; moreover it was in sharpest contrast to the usual policy of the college. Interestingly enough, this deviation from sound practice did not arise from some wealthy patron or trustee who sought to dominate a situation; to have a faculty member exert financial pressure was unique.

Such a defeat for the trustees arose from the unwisdom of the president in stressing unduly his frustration in dealing with poor teachers, when for the governing board to do anything drastic was certain at that stage to make matters worse, not better. The secondary effect was more important than the primary, as is often the case. The trustees, balked in their negative action, decided upon a "positive" approach. They took advantage of an interim situation, while an acting president served as *locum tenens*, to provide a bonus for specially good teaching. Surely this was a sound idea and one now widely in use. The notion that salaries should be level for everyone of the same age and grade, without any regard for quality of instruction or scholarly research, denies all reality. Unfortunately in this instance the trustees sought to paint the lily; provision was made to review the grant at the end of three years and discontinue it if the recipient's teaching had declined in effectiveness. The stipend was to be transferred to someone whose work seemed more successful at that time.

In principle this was not unsound. Anyone who has taught knows that his effectiveness varies from year to year —sometimes radically. One of the best teachers I ever had swung back and forth between exciting instruction and boring sterility over the twenty years I followed his work closely. The periods of brilliance far outweighed the slumps. What caused this unusually sharp contrast within one man's work no one knew. In principle, I repeat, the idea of a temporary grant has some merit. Its weakness lies in practical application: who is to decide upon the precise degree of excellence at a given moment? That is a task from which, as a president, I would flee. In the case in point the new president who was to administer the plan was thought to be a "trustees' man"; the idea was current that the trustees were going to "cut the faculty down to size." Under these circumstances it looked to many as though the carrot and stick technique was being employed—and faculty members did not fancy themselves as asses.

The upshot was that by the device of the "president's advisory committee" the faculty got tacit, but effective, control of the plan. Except for one or two who declined the bonuses, the special salaries went to senior members of the faculty, and none was withdrawn at the end of the three-year interval. It was another defeat for the trustees; ultimately the scheme was dropped.

The conclusion I drew, and applied to my own procedures, was that the president must be the mediator between trustees and faculty. The two groups have different composition, different tenure, different aims, and differing functions. Yet they must work in harmony so far as may be humanly possible. The president must be honest with trustees about faculty, but he should never say everything that passes through his mind, particularly in moments of fatigue and annoyance. Most trustees are alumni, and they tend, in retrospect, to see "their" faculty through something of a purple haze; "there were giants in the earth in those days." The "new" men (some of whom have been there twenty-five years!) do not seem as majestic or as human or as possessing any one of a dozen other "remembered," but idealized, characteristics. The exposition of the virtues and the rationalization of the idiosyncracies of the current faculty constitute one of the president's chief tasks in dealing with trustees. He must not only build up the faculty; he must give them a build-up with the governing body.

In like manner he must interpret the trustees to the faculty—fully as difficult an enterprise. In this effort he is moving in a highly resistant medium. He must exercise all his powers to prevent either body from trespassing upon the rights, duties, and privileges of the other. He must seek to go further and prevent even the shadow of such infringement. To attain those ends requires the wisdom of Solomon. And, historically, the wisdom of that ancient sovereign would not be so famous if like sapience were more common. The president who does not occasionally feel the pressure from one side or the other—or both—is rare indeed.

The next obligation of a president to his trustees is to find work for them to do, and, even more, appropriate tasks. This is no plea for "busy work," as it used to be called when I was in grammar school. It must be real work. It may seem strange, at first thought, that this should be a president's duty. A moment's reflection makes it clear that it can devolve on no other person. Trustees are unpaid; they have no method of analyzing talents and making assignments. The president is in a position to do so.

College accounting is one such field; it is different from

business accounting. Historically it used to be a mere record to show that money was not stolen; it revealed nothing about waste or maladministration. There was no "budget" as an instrument of management. When large sums are spent, as at present, the accounts need to reflect the uses to which funds are put, and careful interpretation of the accounts reveals the skill, or lack of it, of the principal administrative officers.

When I found a trustee adept in corporate accounting who was ready to take the time and make the effort to comprehend not only the similarities but the differences between that and college accounting, I had a jewel. Under his leadership the "audit committee," which had performed only perfunctorily, was galvanized into life. New auditors were employed, men particularly experienced in educational work. Their analyses and criticisms were reviewed with insight and sound judgment regarding the local situation. The work of that trustee had a permanent effect upon improved management of the institution. Moreover, he was able to interpret college accounting to the other businessmen on the board who had not theretofore understood the difference between business management and business*like* control of a college.

More readily identifiable are investment skills. But even in this field there is need to find men willing to consider the difference between a college endowment and the investments of a trust company, an insurance company, or the reserves of a business corporation. It is relatively easy to find conservators who will "preserve the principal" without much concern for income. It occasionally happens that a trustee who has been a successful speculator wants to handle college funds as he does his own. I served as a trustee of an institution which suffered that kind of speculative control for a time. In the course of discharging various responsibilities I have known plenty of both types. To discover a leader of the investment committee who knows intimately the special needs of a college fund, who has a mind flexible enough not to use inappropriate rule-of-thumb principles, yet is not a speculator—that is a task. If the president puts his mind to it and works closely and in harmony with such a man he will "make" money, which he will then not have to "raise."

A good chairman of a building committee is equally hard to find, but when one is discovered he can save money, get better buildings, and take a load off the president's back. It is romantic to think it is possible to select an architect and turn the designing over to him alone; moreover it is unfair to him. A good architect deserves a good owner. He can seldom give a college something desirable in a building that the institution does not know it wants. A president should hang over the drawing boards until he is able to read a blueprint; he should call attention to classroom doors opposite each other in a corridor—guaranteeing a crush between classes. But he has other duties.

A trustee who has wide experience in building, who knows materials, who will not make a "saving" in construction that will be lost many times over in costlier maintenance—such a man can mean many thousands of dollars to the college. He is likely to give services far beyond his capacity to donate money of equal value. Moreover, he is in a position to interpret the president's aims to the board in terms that they, as businessmen, will understand and accept from him, whereas some of them will be skeptical of the practical sense of an "educator." The president may be right, but if he is not believed he might almost as well be wrong. An interpreter is often essential.

Problems of insurance, landscaping, maintenance, the library, the athletic plant—and dozens, not to say hundreds, more—provide an opportunity for trustees to work for the college. Getting them to do something educates them in their real function. A famous university business officer spoke of some committee meetings as "among the most valuable and interesting seminars in a university." Such instruction keeps trustees alert as no amount of reports, exhortations, or oratory can do; it also keeps them "shinnying on their own side," leaving the faculty to perform its reasonable service.

It is essential, within the limits of practicality, to spread these assignments among as many members of the board as possible, else the cry will be raised that a "ring" is in control—"the rest of us are just dummies," an excuse to take no responsibility. I have before me an instance. In a board which is very large there are over ten standing committees; but a quarter of all the assignments are in the hands of six men, and another thirty percent in those of nine others. Fifteen out of sixty hold half the assignments. Is it any wonder the full board is not very active?

A secondary result follows this concentration. Attendance at committee meetings is frequently very poor; it averages about fifty percent in one university. Those who have too many assignments cannot give enough time to attend all the meetings; indeed it transpires that there are often conflicting dates. Those who feel they are "outsiders," and "not influential," do not accept any deep responsibility for attendance. This leads to what I have found, over the years, to be one of the most frustrating experiences for a president—a variable quorum.

At one session a matter is presented, discussed fully, and acted upon. At the next meeting a different quorum is present; a man absent from the previous session does not understand what transpired and wants the whole matter dealt with *de novo*. Other former absentees join in the request and what was once "settled" must be re-presented, re-argued, re-decided. Often the new decision is not identical with the earlier one. Whereupon a member of the first quorum, but not the second, raises the question "What gives?" at the next meeting. Under such circumstances—all too frequent in large boards with inadequate attention to committee assignments—the business of the college stutters.

As pointed out earlier, the president should serve *ex officio* on all committees and attend as many as he possibly can. When he cannot be present he should send another administrative officer who is familiar with the whole range of policies, and who should report to him promptly and fully. Modern institutions are so big and so complex that centrifugal forces are powerful. To bring, if not unity, at least coherence to policy requires someone at each committee meeting to see that it does not fly off at a tangent. President Harnwell of the University of Pennsylvania expressed it well: "The university presents so many facets to society that it is often not recognized as a single entity, even by those within it." It was in an effort better to counteract the centrifugal forces within universities that the Association of American Universities was reorganized about a decade ago. It has not been nearly so successful in accomplishing this objective as was hoped.

Committee meetings give the president an opportunity to explain his proposals in a more informal and intimate manner and answer questions no one would raise in a big meeting. They also supply the best occasion to feel the pulse of the trustees. Irritations with him or his policies are revealed which tend to be suppressed when the full board is in session. To a president aware of the political character of his office, that opportunity to sense the atmosphere within his governing body is important.

One rule in dealing with trustees I found almost essential: when I asked for advice I took it, even when it was unpalatable. I tried to select a man or woman whose judgment regarding the subject in hand was worthy of respect; then I followed it. The rule had a corollary: when the advice was accepted the responsibility for the decision was mine. It should never be thrown back on the unpaid counselor, else his readiness to put his mind on a college problem would be impaired. A president who does not accept responsibility for all decisions even when they are taken reluctantly, on advice, is not facing up to his job.

This was brought home to me when the war imperiled the survival of most fraternities at Brown. I made some tentative recommendations for their salvation at a meeting of the corporation. During a luncheon break three fellows and two trustees, all of whom had had sons at Brown at about that time, were discussing my proposals when I joined the group. They were agreed, unanimously, that they would not accept the suggestions I had made, and began to develop alternatives. I participated but little, and bent my energies to listening. They worked out a proposal radical in form and substance, and I omitted lunch to dictate their conclusions while they were still fresh in my mind.

That draft was laid before the Advisory and Executive Committee of the corporation at two successive monthly meetings, and modified in several particulars. Only then was it presented to the full corporation for protracted discussion and action. If ever there was a product of the thinking of many minds, that proposition fulfilled the description. Yet, when adopted, it was "my" plan, and most of the bricks that flew were aimed at me. That is why the president has been called a lightning rod—he must convey the heat safely to the ground without burning the trustees.

This episode was dramatic, but typical. The inner committee which exercises the powers of the corporation between its semiannual meetings is well called the Advisory and Executive Committee. Its executive actions seldom take over thirty or forty minutes of the monthly sessions; the next hour and a half—or more—are truly advisory. Plans still fluid are discussed, modified, discarded, or approved. They are rarely put in final form until a consensus is reached, and I was always ready to go to great lengths to attain one. Nothing is less useful to a president than a closely divided vote or "approval" of a recommendation that is not fully understood—"digested" would be a better word. Such "approval" vanishes when the shooting starts and the most negligent members of the board begin to back out with the feeble excuse: "The president did not make his point clear."

When the chips are down and some really serious issue is raised, boards of trustees usually act not only responsibly, but with courage and firmness. But on issues of lesser import, or if the problem is many sided and hence subject to many conflicting interests and points of view, the timid tend to dominate. They will talk endlessly of "public relations," of the danger of alienating alumni or donors, of losing students. Reflecting upon experience with trustee committees, I am reminded of Parkinson's "Law of Triviality": "the time spent on any item of the agenda will be in inverse proportion to the sum involved," or its importance.

Managing to live with a board of trustees is like riding a spirited horse that is very skittish. Trustees will shy at a shadow rather more quickly than at real danger. Nonetheless, people like to ride spirited horses, and after one has learned the art it is a thrilling experience, and never boring.

In American institutions, with their almost completely decentralized ownership and control, there is no substitute for regents or trustees. I almost wrote "no escape from regents or trustees." In practically every field the expert is subject to supervision by the amateur. Even the commander-in-chief in the United States—the president—is usually a civilian, and has been in all our wars. The corporation executive is responsible to a board of directors. There is no reason why a college president should be in a different position. The solution is one common to many relationships in life: wise definition of function, restraint in the exercise of power, and mutual respect.

III

The Faculty

WHEN I became a college president I was almost serenely confident about one aspect of my work—my relations with the faculty. I had come up through the faculty grades, and knew at first hand how discouraging interviews about "the future" could be. While a professor I had worked in the faculty, and on behalf of the faculty, since better salaries were the prime objectives of the financial campaign. Too heavy a load of teaching I had experienced; too rapid a shift in courses taught I had endured to the point of exhaustion. The pressure of instruction, committee work, community service, and family life as obstacles to research I knew all too well.

The Wesleyan faculty of that day was small; it formed an intimate and extremely warm-hearted society. There were personal animosities within the group, but no cliques or factions. Occasional tensions appeared between older and younger teachers, but they were not serious or of long duration. Save for salaries, which were improving, the situation was as nearly ideal as is likely to prevail in any institution.

In going to Lawrence I proposed to teach, insofar as other duties would permit, and also to complete a major research project upon which I had long been engaged. From my point of view I was moving to another faculty. It would mean developing new friendships and associations, but that seemed a perfectly natural process. The academic profession is, especially for the person under forty, a peregrinating sort of existence; a man seldom teaches in only a single institution. If he is successful—and perhaps more so if he is not—he may well teach in four or five. A move from one to another is therefore not unusual, but rather something to be taken in stride.

Moreover, the committee which nominated me had the active participation and advice of several members of the Lawrence faculty. I had been with those men for several hours, and had also met a considerable number of the professors who were not on the committee. All the contacts had made a favorable impression. I noticed, of course, indications of personal idiosyncracies—but such are part of the stigmata of the academic world. There had been plain justification for the old joke that a professor is a man who thinks otherwise.

On the other hand, I perceived clear evidences of a will and a capacity for mutual accommodation. Among the faculty there had been, for many years, a Jewish rabbi. In order not to trespass upon his Sabbath, the faculty had changed its regular meeting from late Friday to Tuesday. It was striking enough to find a rabbi on the faculty of a college with a strong Methodist tradition and a large number of ministers on its board; it was an even more propitious sign of faculty temper that they had taken pains to make him feel thoroughly at home.

In no matter did the realities prove to be so much at variance with my expectations as in the relationship with the faculty. Problems resulted in part from a circumstance that is quite common, but every president believes he is the only sufferer. This was recalled to my mind when, not too long ago, I was visiting a new university president. He had made an extraordinarily good start and the institution gave every indication of prosperity under his leadership. As I congratulated him on this auspicious situation he fell silent, then he asked if I had ever had the experience of having to live and work with a candidate for the office who failed to be chosen. I found myself making the conventional remarks, forgetting my own experience over a generation ago.

When I returned home memory stirred, and I was able to tell him a good deal more. Indeed, my arrival at Lawrence found at least two men who felt they should have been chosen. One, a close administrative colleague, had been in theological seminary with my father. This created a personal situation of the greatest delicacy. No two people could have been less well suited to work together; not only in age, but in temper, interest, and point of view we were poles apart. Yet we had to remain in daily association for more than half my tenure. His irenic disposition eased personal relations; however nothing could make us effective cooperators. Consequently, I had to get done by others as much as possible of the work he would normally have performed.

The other man was of a different stripe altogether. He had in mind for the college a program the precise opposite of what I was seeking to achieve. Beneath superficial amiability was a hostility which was palpable. He sought to interest me in setting up a new division, giving him the deanship and a free hand. When I declined with great firmness and finality, he resigned to accept a professorship in an institution without good academic standing. But the transition was played up as a great promotion for him and a great loss for Lawrence. That was all right with me; he could make everything possible of the move, so far as I was concerned. Not only did his resignation relieve me of a discontented professor, it opened the way for a clean sweep of the department—and shortly the abolition of its most closely affiliated department also. As the result of new appointments an exceedingly strong department was developed and maintained during the next twenty-five years.

These episodes were trying, but the problems in the relationship with the faculty had deeper roots. They arose from the tradition of the office at Lawrence. My predecessor was a president in the classical tradition. It is hardly too much to say that he was the college. The pervasiveness of his control is symbolized by an occurrence on the last day in the office before his sudden death. A member of the faculty was consulting the president on some academic matter of first importance. In the midst of the conference there was a knock at the door, it opened, and the scrub woman poked her head in to ask, "Which floor shall I wash next?" This detailed supervision carried over into the grave. Soon after I arrived, the dean's wife came to me in some distress. She was managing a large tea in one of the dormitories and the matron refused to move an ornate punch bowl "because Dr. Plantz put it on that table and said it was to stay there"! It required my personal, and very firm, interposition to alter its location even temporarily. That was no isolated instance; it was fairly typical.

He had carried the whole enterprise around in his head. The late Chancellor Capen of the University of Buffalo might well have had Dr. Samuel Plantz in mind when he wrote: "The trustees were the sovereigns and the president was their viceroy: a viceroy with full regal powers, since the sovereigns seldom visited their realm. In the president's hands were the high justice, the middle, and the low. He controlled teachers, students, and curriculum. He managed the property. He carried on all the official correspondence of the college and wrote most of its documents, generally with his own hand. He spoke for the college, preached to it, begged for it, thought for it, and castigated its members young and old for their own good. His word was law within the institution. . . . The job, though arduous, was possible for a man of strength and erudition and self-confidence as long as colleges were small and as long as one mind might roughly compass the field of learning embraced in the college curriculum."

There was benevolence in this vast authority, accumulated over thirty years. Naturally the faculty, having known no other sort of administration, looked on me as authority personified. But I had not the knowledge, the experience, or the temperament to attempt so much, and delegated as many duties as possible. A snicker went round when Dr. Plantz's small grandson visited the office and remarked proudly, "It takes four people now to do what grandpa did alone."

His observation had the naive acuity of children. I did not resent the ill-concealed laughter, for I had seen the same changes at Wesleyan and knew that the day of one-man management was done. No one could any longer do at Harvard what Charles W. Eliot had done. It was recounted, for example, that on one occasion, when a repair was to be made, he told a carpenter that there was an unused door in the basement of Sever. Nothing was alien to his attention. No one could compass the duties undertaken by William Rainey Harper at Chicago or manage Wisconsin as had Charles R. Van Hise. No more could I do at Lawrence, though it was small, what President Plantz had done so long and so well.

Nevertheless, the aura of authority hung over my office and it made a vast difference. I was no longer just a person, but an officer—with powers which seemed vast to others, however slender they appeared to me. When the first faculty member, half again my age, addressed me as "sir," my surprise was equaled only by my distress. On the volley ball court, or playing tennis, or throwing a basketball I was once again a human being. But in the office the curse of status was laid upon me.

In the thirty years I held office I never got used to the clammy handshake or to seeing the perspiration start out on a man's brow merely because we were discussing college matters. Fear on the part of students always left me sad, for as a professor my contacts with them had been as natural and informal as could be imagined. I had been known as a friend of the rogues, and I must admit I enjoyed some of the rascals a lot more than I did the solemn grinds who never gave the faculty any trouble.

Everything that I could think of I did to overcome the tensions so evident on the part of many—not all, of course —who came to my office on business. The most successful means was to fit up my office like a living room, with comfortable chairs, some plants, a few books and pictures. And I made it a rule not to sit at a desk when conferring with a member of the faculty. Somehow sitting in comfortable chairs, across the room away from desk and telephone, lightened the atmosphere. At Brown the only desk in the public office was an antique slant-top which had belonged to the first president, James Manning; his tall clock stood in the corner. I had a separate small office on a remote floor for desk work.

Another device helped ease official relations. Often a member of the faculty had a minor problem which was none the less irritating. Such problems might have been inflated beyond their due by a formal appointment; so I let it be known that there was tea at four each afternoon. Many a small matter was handled briefly in the relaxed atmosphere of social intercourse.

As often as possible, instead of meeting in my office, I went to the professor's office to talk about matters in which he had an interest, particularly if equipment or building alterations were involved—things which could best be tackled on the spot. Whenever this was practical, it had a good effect. The professor was on his own ground, in his own familiar place of authority. It increased his confidence and relaxed official tensions.

Sometimes this sense of local proprietorship on the part of the professor created friction—and a good deal of heat. The botany professor claimed that the low humidity of his overheated laboratory impaired his specimens. Thereupon he ordered from "his" funds, i.e. the departmental appropriation, an elaborate humidifying system at heavy cost. Routinely the order came across the desk of the new business manager. He declined to approve it, on the ground that the apparatus would use eight hundred gallons of water every hour without raising the humidity significantly. The professor was brilliant, but volatile. He flared like a Roman candle; his protests were vigorous to the point of violence. This was ignorant administrative interference with his professional judgment; it was bureaucratic obstruction of work necessary for efficient instruction; it was the department's money and must be spent in accord with its judgment (he was the department)—and so on and so forth.

I was in a box. It was essential to support the authority of the new business manager; it was equally necessary to calm the excited professor. The first thing to do was to shift the scene from the administrative offices to the laboratory. I went to the science building and listened carefully to the proposals, inspected the dried up mosses, and pleaded for a few moments of quiet to think, which were not accorded. Then I discussed the matter with the business manager, made it clear I would support him, but urged discovery of a way to ease the crisis. He found one. Calling in the contractor who was selling the humidifying system, the business officer announced flatly that the equipment was no good. He deliberately roused the man to fury and then proposed a test: install the equipment, put in a sealed recording hygrometer which would be opened only in the presence of all the parties at interest; if the humidity went up two points, the full list price was to be paid. Otherwise nothing would be paid. The violence of the contractor's protestations had been so great that he was in no position to refuse.

The upshot was farcical. All the elaborate apparatus was installed, the hygrometer was placed in a position agreed upon by all, the water was turned on like a cataract and sounded like one. In a week of operation absolutely nothing happened. The passage of students, the frequent opening and closing of doors—and the inefficiency of the elaborate contraption—left the humidity virtually unchanged.

The professor had his "system." The mosses continued to dry. No bill was paid. The authority of the business manager was established. Then a small chamber was set up where humidity control was simple and cheap. As a reminder, the pipes and evaporators of the expensive installation were left on the walls through two subsequent paintings and removed after the professor and the business manager had become fast friends.

The boundaries between academic privilege and administrative discretion are ill-defined. I suspect they will always be vague. But they are full of booby traps of the most unexpected kind. A peaceful passage on an innocent occasion may set off a series of incidents painful in the extreme—and sometimes dangerous.

Grades can supply an example. I had an experience during my very first teaching as a "section hand" at Harvard. One of my students, the son of a prosperous industrialist, was getting failing grades. An assistant to the freshman dean called me to the office to talk about the boy. My attention was invited to the fact that he had asthma. Admitting ignorance on that point, I invited attention to the fact that to my certain knowledge he had no history. I was reminded that if I failed him he would be dismissed from Harvard. Naturally that was said in tone of voice as though it were a fate worse than death. So I resorted to Dean Charles H. Haskins, the head of the course. He listened with patience to my recital of the facts, and asked: "Did it ever occur to you that it might be a kindness to the boy to drop him from Harvard?" This was a revolutionary idea, but struck me, in the instance at hand, as a sound one. I failed the student; he was dismissed. He then entered another institution, graduated, and, so far as I know, lived happily ever after.

I had a second experience of a similar nature during the same period. The dean's office informed me that the distribution of the grades I had submitted did not conform to what was then known as the "Harvard curve." Again I laid my troubles before Dean Haskins. With the same patience displayed before he read all the papers to which I had given high grades. In each instance he specifically approved my mark and told me to pay no attention to any administrative complaint. I was free to refer any who objected to him; he and I both knew no officer would think of going so far.

My next experience with grade pressures from administrative sources was as an observer—with mingled amusement and rage. One of the conspicuously poor teachers at Wesleyan preceded me in the use of a large lecture room. He was a man always a little behind in his schedule. He would reach his classroom at the last possible second, except when students sneaked down and locked the back door through which he usually entered. Then, while he fussed with his keys or circumnavigated the building, the magic moment of tolerance passed, the students rushed out, gave the "yell" always accorded a professor who "cut" his class, and dispersed.

Similarly, he did not leave the room when the class was over. Students found that "questions" improved his estimate of them. The marginal gang clustered about the desk like flies; it was the easiest way to get a good grade. As he toiled through dreary answers, time ran out. So I set up a lectern over by the window and began my lecture while he stuffed the books he always carried as excess baggage into the well-known green cloth bag that showed a man had once been at Harvard, and scuttled out. At semester end his grades were so scandalously high that the dean, ordinarily a tolerant man, declined to accept them.

The solution was a piece of utter academic nonsense. The learned professor proceeded to the office, averaged each boy's grades in the other courses taken that semester, and turned in that average as the grade in his course. The rest of the faculty was divided between fury and laughter.

Such was my background on administrative review of grades when I reached Lawrence. Inevitably, being interested in standards, I wanted to find out as much as possible about the grades given there. Consequently I took the registrar's books and studied the entries by every statistical device I could command. It took no profound mastery of technique to discover, beyond doubt, that the basis of grading was sometimes quixotic.

Of course, quixotism and irrelevance in determining "achievement" were not wholly new to me. As a young instructor at Wesleyan I heard one of the stories about Woodrow Wilson's career as a member of that faculty. As commencement approached the whole faculty considered the readiness of each boy for a degree. One senior had clearly failed to meet all the requirements and the faculty was ready to vote against his graduation when one member made an emotional appeal based upon the fact that the student's mother, who lived in Oregon, was already on the train, headed for Middletown. Rather than disappoint her the degree was voted. Wilson hated irrelevancy but bided his time. The next doubtful case was discussed, and at length a vote was called for. At that point Wilson intervened saying that one aspect of the young man's academic qualifications had been withheld from the faculty. The president was clearly nonplused and said, "I am sure, Professor Wilson, we will be glad to supply the deficiency if you will identify it." Whereupon with utmost gravity Wilson inquired, "Has he a mother residing at a distance?"

In my own time the whole faculty still discussed borderline cases. One such was the college messenger, who earned his room by carrying intracampus mail. He was a familiar figure to us all—and so cross-eyed as to be conspicuous. In his last semester he failed to achieve "proficiency" in German. Discussion was long and heated. Meanwhile the instructor involved sat silent, for it was a custom more sacred than a rule that no one of that rank spoke unless requested. Finally a professor suggested that Dr. Stevens's opinion be asked. He was a brilliant man, given to sardonic humor and clearly weary of the long debate. "Well, Mr. President," he said, "it is my considered opinion that his strabismus is so acute that it is unreasonable to expect him to see all the way from one end of a German sentence to the other." On that sally, the lad graduated. Surely I was accustomed to irrelevance, but my sense of humor was not strong enough to accept quixotism as a steady diet.

My study of the Lawrence grades led to serious consideration of the question, "What are marks supposed to measure, or to indicate?" Obviously it was desirable to do something; it was equally clear that any direct or vigorous approach would raise so many hackles that the improvement in grading might well be more than offset by the deterioration in my relationship with faculty members.

Fortunately, at about the time I felt somewhat desperate, a Midwest university published a study of factors taken into account when a grade was assigned. Sixteen different items were included in the list, starting with the only valid criterion—achievement—and running through "attitude toward teachers," attendance, application, deportment, personality, and a whole series of irrelevancies. Each instructor was asked to express, in percentage, the value he put on any item in making up the grade he reported to the registrar. When all the answers were in, a faculty meeting was called to discuss the matter. Some of the strongest professors made the point that achievement was the only proper basis for a college grade. Each member of the faculty had his own answer before him and could draw his own conclusions. No one was publicly humiliated; some told me privately that they were both astonished and ashamed.

Administrative guidance in the matter of grading is occasionally essential. I have known professors to fail a student on an essay examination when he "missed the passing grade by a single percentage point." It has been demonstrated times without number that no such precision is possible. But when an attempt is made to apply any sort of corrective, it must be as impersonal, as statistically obvious, and as confidential as possible.

Whatever the effort at improvement, the president may be well assured that the margin of error will remain wide. And students remember real or fancied injustices a very long time. In my sophomore year a professor (one of the three poor teachers mentioned earlier) gave me a grade below what I felt I had earned. That would have been forgotten soon, but without any protest from me he offered an explanation so utterly silly that it has stayed with me to this day.

And I have been on the receiving end of student expressions of wrath. In my very first class was a student to whom I gave an A grade for the year. He has gone on to a very distinguished scholarly career. When he received his first advance in the academic hierarchy, I chanced to meet him in the library of the university where he was teaching. Full of good will I went up and congratulated him warmly. His response was exceedingly cool and I thought he might have forgotten me and mentioned my name. "How could I forget?" he demanded. "You are the fool who gave me a D at Thanksgiving." That temporary grade, which never went on his record, had rankled for nearly ten years. I have often wondered whether the "D at Thanksgiving" was a measure of his slow adjustment to college, or of my slow progress in mastering the art of teaching. Perhaps it was a little of both.

Poor grading is only one aspect—almost a minor aspect—of inadequate teaching. My experience at Wesleyan had convinced me that incompetent instruction should not be tolerated. Between the time of my graduation from college and my return as an instructor occurred one of the types of explosion that produced the American Association of University Professors, of which I was an early member and have been an honorary member since giving up a professorship for administrative work. As is the case in most such episodes, the professor insisted he was "fired," the president asserted that he had resigned. Both were correct; the teacher resigned under what he conceived to be presidential pressure.

At the moment of the detonation both men were so angry that their judgment and discretion were completely in abeyance. Both said utterly absurd things to each other. Any partisan could make out a case for his side. And, of course, both were wrong. The man had once been a first-class teacher, but had quit serious learning a decade before; he was putting his energies into politics rather than scholarship. His grades had become so erratic the students insisted he threw the papers downstairs, sent his dog to retrieve them, and graded them in the order of their return. This was probably exaggerated.

For his part the president became upset at a remark I had heard the professor make in class at least twenty times. *Bons mots* in the academic world are apt to be iterative. It was a silly statement of what the professor was pleased to call "a strong case for the purposes of the argument." If the president had not heard of it before, it must have been because of his frequent absences and preoccupation with fund raising. He must have been the only campus figure who was not inured to it.

The professor did not suffer unduly. He was "taken care of" by a temporary appointment at Harvard (where the out-of-date nature of his data was soon apparent) and then spent the rest of his life as the dean of an important school in a very large university. The president survived the fireworks, scorched, but not fatally. The damage was to the reputation of the only innocent party—the college. It was many years before instruction in that department was as good as the students deserved. The "hot" vacancy was filled by one of the trio of poor teachers who parade across these pages—and my memory—so frequently.

When I became a president, I knew well what not to do. Never move in a hurry, much less upon impulse. Never get angry; if possible use such temperate language as to give no occasion to the other man to blow his top. He may, but at least furnish no reasonable occasion. I was convinced that no help was to be had from the American Association of University Professors. Early in its history it had stated that the profession should take responsibility for getting rid of the lazy, the incompetent, the unfit. But it never developed any adequate program or procedure for so doing. Its main effort was in protecting professors from presidents and trustees.

The procedures developed for that purpose are so involved that they are not regularly used. Their fatal flaw is that they require a man's colleagues to take an open position. In a small college, the faculty is almost a family. Members will not take an adverse position regarding one of their number in public. Furthermore, a man dismissed after formal charges and "trial" is severely damaged, if not ruined. When he is displaced quietly, he may do well in other circumstances—having learned his lesson. I never resorted to any formal hearing procedure, being convinced it would not work and that, if it did, the consequences for the individual would be needlessly cruel.

In the course of thirty years I displaced no less than five men with tenure; four were full professors. It was done without a fuss with the American Association of University Professors. The method was simple in the extreme. I first checked—in confidence—with the man's colleagues, one at a time. In that way I got candid appraisals. Furthermore, no one heard anything said by a colleague that he could tell his wife, who would repeat it only to her best friend—until it was all over the campus. Second, I promised my advisers that they would not be brought into any unpleasantness; the full responsibility was mine and would remain undivided whatever happened. In the first two or three instances I journeyed to Washington and discussed the whole problem frankly and fully with W. W. Cook, then the executive officer of the Association.

Those steps having been taken—over a considerable period of time so that there could be no shadow of appearance of impulsiveness, I then met the professor—not in the office, or where we could be observed if the going got rough, setting tongues wagging. We met in my home in the evening. In each case I offered a year's leave at full pay, and in one case two years, in exchange for a resignation. The tone was calm, but exceedingly firm.

I had far less trouble in getting the professors to agree to resign than in getting the trustees to authorize such "extravagant" termination payments. For my part, I insisted it was a cheap price; in the long run some who had protested most vigorously came to agree with me. The college should pay some money since the error lay not alone with the professor; the responsibility rested, to some extent at least, with those who had not relieved him of his appointment before he attained "permanent" tenure.

Timidity in deciding not to reappoint a man on term status is one of the worst evils in administrative practice. Often, perhaps usually, the initial difficulty lies with the unwillingness of the department chairman to make up his mind about the man. With the scholar's passion for waiting until all the evidence is in, he postpones decision. But the difference between scholarship and administration lies precisely at that point. The administrator faces deadlines; he must act on the evidence available. As a scholar, no one could hurry me; I wrestled with problems until I was completely convinced before taking a position. As administrator, no such luxury was available; there comes a time of decision. When the chairman will not make up his mind, the president should appoint a new chairman, or himself make the negative decision not to reappoint. Tenure is too vital a treasure to be attained by adverse possession.

Nonreappointment is not tragic when accompanied with early decision; it may become so when action is too long postponed. The academic profession, being as peripatetic as it is, can fit a man into his proper post if given time. It is no unkindness to decline to reappoint a young man, provided he is notified far enough in advance to permit him to find a new position.

One interview, now a quarter of a century back, lingers in my mind. A generous donor to the college was not a trustee; indeed he was chairman of the board of another college, to which he also gave largely. He came to my office to say that at the onset of the depression the college for which he had more direct responsibility had adopted the policy of not displacing any faculty personnel, since jobs were so hard to find. He stated frankly that at the time he had felt critical of me for pursuing a contrary policy. However, he had observed that those who were displaced at Lawrence found posts and did not suffer undue hardship. "The consequence," he continued, "is that our faculty now needs a thorough overhauling, while yours is fresh and well balanced." Such kind words persist in the mind of a president; they are rare enough.

My record is far from flawless. One of the full professors I should have got rid of, I did not, leaving that tough assignment to my successor. The reason was simple. When there was a proper occasion and adequate grounds for action early in my administration, I did not know how to proceed. I was too green and inexperienced to have developed the methods which later worked well. While I held office no second chance was vouchsafed me in his case.

People have often asked if displacements, whether of those on tenure or those with term appointments, do not cause permanent hatred. In some cases they do—as does any responsible decision in matters of personnel. But the rule is the contrary, at least so far as my experience goes. Many who were disappointed or even bitter at the moment subsequently expressed their gratitude and displayed the friendliest feelings. When a man is well placed he is glad to have been stimulated, not to say forced, to find a new position. It is no kindness to keep shoving a square peg into a round hole. Nonreappointment is no final judgment upon the character, talents, or industry of an instructor; it is merely a decision that at that time and place and in those circumstances someone else might meet the situation better. Subject to behaving in a humane manner, the more objective the president's point of view the better—for the college, the appointee, and subsequent good feeling.

At one time (it may have continued since) there was a kind of compact between the Association of American Colleges and the American Association of University Professors and an arrangement for mediation. President McConaughy held the post for some years and I succeeded him in the assignment. During my term as mediator I never defended a teacher who was worthy of consideration personally; it was necessary to uphold principle on behalf of an individual who, as a man, did not merit so much attention. Equally, I never dealt with an administration that was courageous, candid, and deft. Good teaching and good administration would have prevented every single difficulty serious enough to come to our notice. However, all the troubles were settled without academic warfare, avoiding "censure" or other desperate expedients.

As the college president must shape the board of trustees, so in a more direct way he is responsible for the make-up of the faculty. In a small college this is a significant portion of his task. There is no departmental structure adequate to manage its own concerns. There is not enough money to send members of the faculty out scouting and to bring in a series of candidates at college expense. In my eleven years at Lawrence, faculty recruitment was one of the most arduous and time-consuming duties.

There was no easy way to do the job. It required travel to the universities, the development of trustworthy contacts, and careful screening of possibilities. One means of elimination was easy; whenever, as too often happened, the recommendation read, "he has not the scholarly capacity for appointment at a strong university, but will be an acceptable teacher in a college," it ended further consideration of his appointment. This evaluation reflected the unspoken—and often unconscious—contempt of the university professor for colleges. If a man felt that way about a whole group of institutions, his judgment on suitable personnel was not likely to be sound.

A college is not a poor university; it is a different sort of institution. But its standards of instruction and achievement may be just as high as those of a university. Many colleges do, on the whole, better teaching than many universities, even famous ones. A good college is a wonderful place for a man to develop the art of teaching. He will not find it possible to start out as a narrow specialist; he will have to teach courses beyond the confined limits of his particular interest. By so doing, he will vastly increase the range of his learning, for no student progresses so rapidly as an instructor. If he does his work perceptively he will gain a perspective upon his specialty that he might never acquire in a university environment. Moreover, his other urgent preoccupations will furnish a test of his scholarly zeal for research.

It will be said, and with much truth, that the colleges lack equipment equal to that of universities in libraries, laboratories, and financial resources. It will also be argued, with some justice, that many colleges do not have a research atmosphere, that there are not the invisible but potent pressures toward research that characterize some universities. On the other hand, if a man or woman has the root of the matter in him, if he has the inquiring mind, the industry and imagination to do research, he will not be stopped.

I remember vividly, while on a search for talent, a visit to a small college. In a laboratory which seemed to me not much better than an old-fashioned kitchen, interesting and productive research was afoot. The professor involved subsequently held two other academic appointments. In each case the equipment and resources were very much better. His work grew correspondingly in range and depth. But in that first appointment he had shown and developed his mettle.

Indeed, I do not hesitate after all these years of observation to assert that, if the instructor has the essence of scholarship in him, no obstacle will prevent him from useful research. That declaration is no plea for making matters hard in order to test determination; there are enough hazards under the best of conditions. Every college president should improve the equipment, the environment—and the resources. But he must not expect the work done in a new laboratory necessarily to be commensurately better than in the old. Men and women make the difference. Furthermore, every college president should rid himself of the deceptive cliché that research and teaching do not go together. In my experience, taking into account the normal number of exceptions, the rule runs the other way.

The search for first-class teachers and scholars for college instruction is likely to have a corollary: there will be considerable turnover. Those who produce and teach well will have offers to go elsewhere, and many will go. To me this was never a matter of regret. Individuals, of course, sometimes proved irreplaceable, but that is true in universities and in life generally. The significant fact was that the college had the benefit of youth, enthusiasm, energy, ambition, all helpful in making a superior teacher even before experience has matured—or staled—him. A careful study conducted a number of years ago by one of the professional associations gave strong indication that young teachers are often the best—perhaps too often.

The fact that some of a president's best talent discoveries will be lost to the college in due time lays on him a special duty already mentioned: he must weed out those who do not fulfill their promise. Otherwise, as the members of the faculty grow older, he will find that an adverse selection is operating; the best will leave, the poorest will stay. Only the most rigid insistence upon performance standards before tenure is granted can prevent a decline in over-all effectiveness from occurring. This is one of the principal tragedies of the all too prevalent short tenure of presidents; no long-range faculty plan can be followed. And nowhere in college work is the long view so essential as in the selection, the retention, or the discarding of faculty.

A university president faces many of the same dilemmas and decisions as the head of a college. But his relationship to the task is markedly different. He cannot do much recruiting personally. There are too many appointments to be made. Openings are too specialized in their demands for one man to be competent to discover candidates and make sound choices. The sheer bulk and complexity of the undertaking require decentralization among the department chairmen. On appointments of "promising" men and women the president should meet the candidates, form some impression of their adaptability, search out their prejudices, find out if they are perennially discontented—in short, make such observations as an officer experienced in personnel problems generally can make.

This is all very well and works out admirably when a department is strong and the chairman alert to the point of being aggressive. Therefore, it is essential that the president put his thought and energy into developing strong chairmen. That sentence was easy to write, but to give it meaning requires will, persistence, courage, and skill. Some chairmen like to think of themselves as "head" of the department. They acquire a proprietary interest in it; the members of the faculty in that department are "my men" to the chairman. However, permanent heads should be avoided; men get tired after a while. When tired they are apt to be arbitrary. They also get into ruts, recruiting their new staff from a narrow range of institutions.

The problem is to make a change without a row. Often a good chairman likes relief; he will suggest it himself. When that occurs, a number of changes can be made. Sometimes the strongest man does not want to be chairman; he is proof that it is not necessary to be chairman to maintain one's prestige. The best device that I found was a formula which stated that neither the appointment as chairman nor the substitution of another was to be regarded as an expression of approval or disapproval of the manner in which the department had been administered; it was a routine assignment of duties for the time being—in the nature of a committee assignment. But no device, no formula will assuage the feelings of the oversensitive. Yet every time I timidly shrank from making a change the consequences were undesirable. In university administration of a faculty the maintenance of a corps of strong chairmen is a major—not a routine—obligation.

The really frustrating experience is to try to strengthen a weak department with two or three senior faculty members in it. They will not seek out prospects likely to put them in the shade. Other universities discourage their best new products from applying for or even accepting a position. Even if a strong appointment is made, it is likely to be transitory—the eager young instructor wants more stimulating colleagues.

The president may take the bull by the horns, go out and find a good man and appoint him as chairman. This drastic procedure may occasionally succeed, but in most instances is not likely to work well. The departmental colleagues of the "president's pet" will accept him reluctantly, if not resentfully. They will find ways to drag their feet. This may be their natural pace; the process need not be malicious. The "outsider" is made to feel himself an outsider. If he becomes an insider, he tends to sink toward the local level. More likely he gets out.

In thirty years I tried many gambits to strengthen weak departments. I was still trying when I retired. But it must be confessed that the only device that worked with any consistency was to keep the weak department fluid with term appointments until the unsatisfactory "leaders" retired. Sometimes retirements could be accelerated. Then a fresh start was possible.

In both college and university the problem of faculty retirement policy is one of the president's main responsibilities. I had seen at first hand the tragedy of retirement postponed too long. One of my most distinguished teachers, widely recognized as a man of unusual skill, came to the retirement age. I joined with many others of the faculty in urging him to continue teaching. He acceded reluctantly. Then in the midst of a semester the tragedy unfolded. His powers had declined; the new generation of students knew little of his great tradition. They were aware of his failing capacity and, with the thoughtless savagery of youth, made his life utterly miserable. A career that should have ended on a high note was brought to a wretched conclusion.

When I reached Lawrence the retirement policy was not

established. My predecessor managed such things according to his judgment; but I did not have the experience, the perspective, the intimate knowledge of the men to follow his course. As a consequence, a fixed age of retirement was set by the trustees, on my recommendation. There was provision for possible extensions, but I announced that there would be no extensions in the foreseeable future.

This produced some painful, and some farcical, episodes. One professor who for many reasons, including health, should have been the first to desire retirement resisted it most violently. He came into my office, and in solemn, not to say sepulchral, tones said: "Retirement will kill me, and as I approach the end, I'm going to insist on being carried to your doorstep, there to die and show what you have done." He retired, lived happily to a ripe old age. Long after I left Lawrence and went to Brown he kept up a friendly—and exceedingly voluminous—correspondence. In the fullness of years he ultimately died thirty-five hundred miles from my doorstep.

Another instance did not work out so happily. One of those who faced retirement was well-to-do and had a remunerative consulting business. His colleagues were in no doubt that he should retire. But he never willingly spoke to me again. If we were forced together he would be polite, but with a wounded look in his baby-blue eyes that I can still see.

Later on, with greater experience, I pursued a more flexible policy. In retrospect, however, I must confess that when I made an error it arose from hesitation to face the interview that seems so much like putting an end to a man's professional career. In practice the actual "end to a career" is, in many cases, still some distance off. A teacher who has kept his intellectual vigor and physical vitality often finds temporary appointments. The Whitney Foundation has done wonderful work in this respect. And many small colleges have found great value in from one to three or four years' service of a "retired" professor. A faculty member who retired soon after I went to Brown kept such a "temporary" appointment well over a decade.

Furthermore, improved pension systems have eased the problem significantly. When Andrew Carnegie turned his attention to the issue something over half a century ago, the situation was tragic. The pioneer efforts of his Foundation for the Advancement of Teaching showed that philanthropy, however munificent, could not meet the situation. The Teachers Insurance and Annuity Association, the College Retirement Equities Fund, Social Security, Blue Cross, Blue Shield, group insurance, and many other institutions and devices have been developed. They cannot replace thrift and good judgment; they cannot prevent tragedy. But they can, and do, give the problems of retirement new and more manageable dimensions.

Central to the president's task in administering a faculty is a rational plan. A good department can be wrecked if all its full professors are due to retire almost simultaneously. A poor department may remain poor a long time if inadequate leadership has gained appointments with tenure for weak younger men who will succeed to the chairmanship by accumulated seniority. Young men of promise can be discouraged from remaining if the ranks above them seem crowded. Since the plan has to do with human beings it cannot be merely a formal blueprint. Inasmuch as it deals with many departments whose situations offer sharp contrasts, the plan must be drafted with insight and imagination. The first step is to have full possession of as many facts as possible, available in compact, readily usable form. Judgment requires data.

The best device I was ever able to find was a faculty

pattern book—called, in the office, "the black book." It listed the faculty by age, by grade, by years of service, and of service in each grade, by department—and in every other way that seemed likely to be significant. It made comparisons among colleagues possible, and it is certain that even if the president fails to make such comparisons others will not. The promotion of one teacher when there are others of the same age, grade, and period of service needs to be made in acute consciousness that questions will be asked—overtly or silently—as to whether the discrimination was justified or just a piece of carelessness or favoritism. The consensus of the discontented may be that some aggressive chairman took care of "his" man at the expense of other chairmen less urgent in their recommendations.

It would be a vicious use of such data if teachers were promoted merely by age, or by any other statistical measure. Achievement is the only basis for advancement. I did not hesitate to appoint a few men to full professorships at thirty. Nor did I promote others because of that action. The essential point is that the decision in every instance must be made in conscious awareness of how it will look to others who do not have the same official responsibility but do have strong personal feelings.

The faculty, as a corporate body, needs to have balance. It may come by chance, but the statistical likelihood of such a happy event is negligible. Proper balance is an achievement and demands thoughtful care. Too heavy a concentration of full professors makes it difficult to recruit and keep younger men. Too many instructors give energy and enthusiasm to teaching, but inadequate maturity.

The plan should be made carefully, but it must never become a rigid mold. I served on a group advising another institution about one of its departments which had a large research program. Scrutiny of its work soon revealed projects well conceived and well begun that seemed to wither away and disappear. Inquiry brought the response that the man in charge had gone to another institution leaving the project he had been handling without direction. When three or four such instances turned up, the obvious question was: Why did so many men of unusual promise leave? It transpired that there was a rule of thumb that no promotions with tenure could be made unless there was a vacancy in a post with tenure in the same department. Since this whole enterprise within the institution was fairly new, there were no such vacancies, and therefore no permanent future for even the most brilliant men. I could not help asking myself: "Why should the thumb govern tenure? Why not use the head instead?" Every time a formula is substituted for responsible judgment there is official defeasement. Rules make decision easy but rob it of wisdom.

There will be occasions when, through some accidental circumstance, a first-class man becomes available. Such men and such opportunities are both rare and the conjunction of the two rarer still. Then all dogmas should be discarded. Get the man. A plan is a guide for normal situations; when something unusual supervenes, seize the opportunity and let the plan stay on ice for a while.

Not only should the mold of the plan be broken when rare opportunity presents itself, but fiscal considerations should not dominate the decision to seize the moment or let it pass. American enterprise is supposed to be founded upon risk-taking; the risks should not be rash, but if some are not taken the system is nonsense. Academic advance does not come, for most institutions, without taking chances. Refusal to accept hazards is neither good business sense nor good educational statesmanship.

The boldest move I ever made at Lawrence was the establishment of the Institute of Paper Chemistry. The need for a research and training center for that great industry was clear enough; in 1929 individual companies—with a few conspicuous exceptions—did not appreciate the necessity for fundamental, or even applied, research. Yet such activity was clearly the key to the future. The Fox River Valley was a good place for it, since it was the center of considerable paper manufacturing; with the retreat of the forest line to faraway places the valley industry was faced with adjustment to new circumstances or extinction.

In some ways Lawrence College seemed singularly inappropriate as entrepreneur. It was a liberal arts college; its resources were already strained; its personnel was excellent but fully occupied. On the other hand, there were hidden assets: a trustee had experience, determination, influence, and a willingness to put all those at the service of the venture; a development officer had almost unique promotional skill. Moreover, the college had high—and rising—standards; its staff knew what good work was and would not tolerate shoddy performance.

Clearly, to put the whole institute within the college would lead to severe imbalance—so severe as to impair its devotion to the liberal arts. Therefore, the institute was made an affiliated institution. There was an interchange of faculty and administrative leadership, and a core of trustees was common to both. The whole scheme was put in motion about two weeks before the famous crash of 1929. That the institute has survived and flourished like the green bay tree is the full justification for the risks that were taken —and they were considerable. Its establishment had a marked effect upon the college faculty in many ways. Science departments with small resources had access to larger facilities; groups of men and women with like intellectual interests offer more stimulation than isolated professors can achieve.

At Brown there were two instances where the settled pattern was altered. The first came about through the tyranny of Hitler. One of the great scholars of Germany in the field of mathematical history would not abide it, and went to Denmark. It was soon clear that this haven was not safe. The late Dean R. G. D. Richardson, who all but created the modern graduate school at Brown, suggested we offer him an appointment. There was no "vacancy," there were no surplus resources. But what is a university for if not to be the home of distinguished scholars? So he was invited to come. He left Denmark just before German troops arrived. That appointment led to the establishment of *Mathematical Reviews* in this country, and to a whole series of other consequences of benefit to American scholarship.

The second instance was a more radical deviation from "the plan." Dean Richardson called my attention to a report by Dr. Thornton C. Fry of the Bell Telephone Laboratories on the state of applied mathematics in the United States. It outlined (long before Sputnik) the urgent need for development of centers for study and research in that field. Brown had, traditionally, a strong mathematics department, an outstanding library on the subject, but virtually no work in applied mathematics. Again, there was a distinguished professor available—but he was located in Istanbul.

This was a gamble; no one knew better than I. Early in my experience at Lawrence I made some appointments on the basis of papers, records, recommendations—and with disastrous results. The appointees were so bad that I determined never again to risk a "picture bride." But I did, with great success in the case of Nathan Pusey, as will later appear. This instance was the greatest gamble ever: to bring a scholar half round the world to a permanent position with no interview, no knowledge of the man's adaptability to a new environment or his gifts at developing and managing a new department—for which no funds were in sight. This was academic risk-taking with a vengeance. But Dean Richardson was a good judge of excellence, so the decision was made.

Then began one of those games of hide-and-seek with the government that make influence-peddling understandable—and thriving. The State Department simply would not move to permit the entry of our appointee—or to refuse it. The war had begun in Europe; one route after another for his move to Brown was being closed. The British were cooperative, but from Washington, silence. At last I went to see the Assistant Secretary of State in charge. When I entered his office his desk was absolutely bare—not a paper in sight. He listened courteously to my recital and then said as blandly as you please, "I never heard of him."

The moment had come for desperate measures. I said, "Why not open the top right-hand drawer of your desk and take out the file." With a startled look he did just that, and inquired, "How did you know?" "Well," I said, "the only element of chance lay in whether it was the left-hand drawer, instead of the right." That apparently made it all perfectly clear to him.

His next comment startled me. He said he did not know what applied mathematics was; if I could enlighten him on that point the professor would be admitted. My last mathematics had been as a college freshman, and there was nothing applied about it. Nevertheless, I used every term I had heard used by Dr. Fry and Dean Richardson, made my exposition as long and involved as possible. Whereupon, with a gleam of humanity theretofore hidden by his official pose, he said, "I do not understand that, and, frankly, I don't think you do either. But he can come in." Such is statesmanship. The appointee came with a Czech passport (so far as I know he had never even visited the country) by way of British India. The Applied Mathematics Department at Brown has grown and thrived ever since. It was a risk which fully justified itself.

No one need expect me to detail the breaches of plan that did not work out so well. Into every life some rain must fall, and there were times when I thought I would drown. In retrospect, however, I remain convinced that an essential part of the president's job is long-range planning—if the pattern is not rigid, and if, when unique opportunities come, the risks (academic, fiscal, personal) are accepted.

Dealing with the faculty is serious business, but it does not have to be solemn. Some of the most absurd episodes in all my experience have been in faculty meetings. On one occasion at Wesleyan a member insisted on strict observance of parliamentary procedure. The topic was not vital, but opinion was divided, not between a majority and a minority, but into small fractions. When the matter was presented, one amendment after another was offered, debated, and voted down; then followed a motion to reconsider, also voted down, killing the proposition dead. Each amendment suffered the same fate, then the original proposal was lost, reconsidered, and lost again.

Everyone knew, by that time, where the consensus lay; nearly everyone wanted to find a way to achieve that desired end. But the stubborn parliamentarians dominated and blocked all roads. More in a spirit of fun than anything else I addressed the president and said I had a new matter to present. He recognized me and asked my motion. "I move that when the secretary of the Faculty next prints the catalogue he be instructed to replace the language of paragraph three on page thirty-four as follows" and then used the words of the vote that had come nearest to passage. In a gale of laughter the motion was passed before Robert's Rules of Order could be thumbed through by the sticklers.

Faculty meetings can be deadly, or they can be lively. At

Lawrence I found the atmosphere grim. The practice at Wesleyan was to sit in a big circle, no one in any second row—until the faculty got too large. When addressing the chair or the meeting no one rose; no "speeches" were made. Except on a few sticky occasions such as I have recounted the business was done informally and without ceremonial. My first meeting at Lawrence was set up like a schoolroom —I, the teacher, up front, and the faculty in tablet chairs, row on row. When a man or woman spoke he rose, often came forward, and made a speech. The dullest were the longest. It was at that first meeting that I made up my mind that one brand new member of the faculty (appointed to a full professorship with tenure!) must go. He was not only prolix, but vapid. He subsequently went out on an attempted squeeze play that failed; while I was in the East on vacation he sent a long telegram reporting an offer at another institution which he would accept unless I raised his salary. My response was a telegram accepting his resignation and congratulating him on his new appointment. When he suggested he would rather stay at Lawrence I replied that the matter was closed.

Everything I could think of I did to make faculty sessions less formal, but with only moderate success, and slowly. One of the elder members of the faculty, a first-class teacher, who sent a great many students on to graduate school, was friendly but resisted every change I suggested. He was a blunt man, to the point of being brusque. And in opposition he had a formula I found infuriating: "It may work all right east of the Alleghenies, but not out here in the Middle West." Nothing seemed to have any effect in changing that attitude. Finally I had my sweet revenge. He made a proposal in faculty meeting. Without waiting for discussion I said as bluntly as he was accustomed to do, "It won't work." He had a quick temper, which flared instantly: "Why not?"

"Well," I said, "it works east of the Alleghenies, and since they are such a barrier it won't work here." There was a moment when we were close to an explosion, then with a glint in his eye he said, "I'll take down my half of the Alleghenies if you will take down yours." The mountains were never reerected.

I can recall a number of tense, angry sessions of the faculty when no exercise of tact, no appeal to humor did the slightest good. Professors were in a fighting mood and were determined to fight. Yet, for the life of me, I cannot recall, in a single instance, what the shouting was about. Of this I am sure; it was never about any really significant matter. A campus is like an army camp—rumors fly like the wind. The more improbable they are, the faster they move and the more speedily they gain currency as "true." Unless a president is alert to hear and quick to counter he may find himself in the midst of a synthetic storm of great violence.

I have seen it happen in faculty meetings—and in trustee meetings. In a noted college, not many years ago, the president entered a board meeting. All went serenely for a time; with no hint of warning there was a sudden explosion of pent feelings and he was out of office before the board adjourned. Two or three times in thirty years of presiding over a faculty I have found it expedient to adjourn the session, give time for everyone to cool off, and seek the root of the difficulty, which was seldom the subject matter in hand. That merely furnished the occasion; it was not the cause of the outburst, which had its origin not in reason but in emotion.

Faculty meetings represent the lowest common denominator of the group. Perhaps that is true of all meetings, but at first blush it seems surprising in a body of intellectuals. It must be remembered, however, that even intellectuals are not all-round intellectuals—except in rare instances. They have particularities as well as peculiarities, and all those reveal themselves, often in their worst light, at faculty meetings. For that reason the most careful preparation is desirable; some of it is formal, but the most effective means to peace and progress lies in patient, alert attention to the current mood. When the atmosphere is calm, wonders can be worked; when the barometer is falling, any trivial item on the agenda may precipitate thunder and lightning.

It is not necessary for the faculty to meet regularly more than once a month if the administrative officers, particularly the president, are alert to the atmosphere of opinion. When it does meet, its business can ordinarily be dispatched with brevity and a minimum of waste motion. But there must always be room for the free expression of critical opinion, and no effort should be made to suppress, or even to curtail, it. Often, when the formal business was done, I would ask if anyone had anything to say for the good of the order. Usually the call produced smiles. Occasionally it led to serious discussion. The faculty could then sit two or three hours, if necessary, till the whole matter was thrashed out and the air cleared.

I entered upon my work as president convinced that faculty members should be left alone as much as possible. My own teaching had been made unnecessarily arduous by surplus committee work and academic odd jobs with a maximum of chaff and a minimum of wheat. My point of view as of 1925 is expressed with great pungency by a distinguished professor in Cornell University, Dr. Max Black. "The ideal faculty man, as I have rather romantically been thinking of him, ought properly to find administration distasteful. A man who positively enjoys sitting on committees, arguing about university affairs, or haggling about the wording of regulations, is unlikely to be passionately interested in teaching, scholarship or research." This I believed in 1925 when I began to administer; I believed it even more deeply when I retired in 1955.

The authentic voice of the scholar speaks in the recent novel, *A Friend in Power*, by Professor Carlos H. Baker of Princeton. The central character says: "No more committees, please. I'm on enough committees, as it is. . . . They say it's the price you pay for democratic government in a university. And the places that don't have committee government are always trying to get it. But who pays the price of scholarship? Who writes the books on Shakespeare, Sophocles, Voltaire? No books were ever written while a man sat at a committee table." With too many committees "your scholarly enterprises kept getting the short end of the stick."

An institution should be run democratically; no one should seek to argue that point. The faculty should have control of academic policy. But the routines and the details can be handled by men and women who do not have the creative gifts that true research and first-class teaching require. For that reason I obeyed so far as possible what I called the eleventh commandment, "Thou shalt not commit."

Before our marriage my wife, who was a dean in a famous college, sat on over twenty committees—and that was only a sample among them all. The hours from four to six in the afternoon when a scholar's study is at its best were absorbed, for many of the faculty, in what is essentially administrative work. The cost of this is tremendous, not alone in teaching and research energies lost, but in cash. Unfortunately in college accounting all such labor is listed under instruction, which it certainly is not. If it were charged, on a per hour rate, to administration, which most of it is, the amount would be horrendous.

I was often criticized for expending too much money on administration. One of my colleagues in the faculty at

Brown, who had known me in Harvard, was particularly outspoken in this matter. Then he went to visit the college where he had done his undergraduate work and remained several days on the campus with faculty friends. On his return to Providence he took pains to come in and say, "I will never be critical on that point again. Most of my friends on that faculty are spending an hour or two a day doing things with which I am never bothered here. I appreciate being left alone to teach and do research."

The worst of it is that most committee time is wasted. Members do not usually deal with policy, but discuss specific instances—the admission or non-admission of a particular applicant, whether to grant a scholarship and of what size, or a loan and of what size, or both to an individual whom few, if any, of the committee know. They judge from a piece of paper with his "record."

Some committee work is essential. When a change is to be made in the curriculum the issues are of high academic importance and have a direct bearing upon instruction. Consideration of problems of such magnitude and significance justifies the expenditure of a good deal of time by the best people on the faculty. Moreover, such study is directly related to instruction, and is not properly an administrative cost.

For the rest, there is no sense in substituting the machinery of democracy for its spirit. Yet that is what a great deal of committee government really amounts to. Such waste of scholarly time and effort can be avoided with no loss to genuine democracy, which is a spirit of government, not a mechanism.

A president should keep his ear to the ground, remain alert to faculty criticism or discontent. At the first rumblings he should make a sincere effort to get to the root of the trouble. Usually it is some episode, misunderstood, which has upset an individual who multiplies his discontent by comment at the faculty club or elsewhere. He needs to be seen, and tactfully straightened out. Sometimes the difficulty is due not to misunderstanding but to some real error in judgment on the part of the president or some other administrative officer. That requires quick admission of error and steps to see that it is not repeated. If the matter is of deep significance it should lead to an *ad hoc* committee, a candid airing of the difficulty, and, sometimes, a faculty meeting for a complete exposition of the issue. The faculty meeting is, in the best of circumstances, a gun behind the door. After that the committee men may return to their more rewarding academic labors.

It has been said that a president must develop the hide of a rhinoceros, so that criticism will not irritate him. No statement could be wider of the mark. The key to successful handling of a faculty without wasting their time or the president's lies precisely in sensitiveness to criticism. He should not be so thin-skinned that his primary reaction is to be hurt by every blunt expression of discontent, but he must by no means be so tough as to be callous. The maintenance of the right balance is an art learned, if ever, after many wounds occasioned by inexperience, unwisdom, or plain carelessness. So far as is humanly possible, the president should let the members of the faculty alone, giving them all the freedom practicable for teaching and research. But the relationship is not reciprocal; faculty members have no obligation to leave the president alone. He must be available, responsive—and patient.

Patience is indeed a key word. There is a kind of built-in, automatic resistance to anything a president proposes. I remember talking with a well-known president, universally regarded as "successful," shortly before he resigned. He was telling me, as an old friend, of his mood and what produced it. Conspicuous among the ingredients was the fact, as he expressed it, that "adoption of whatever I suggest is certain to be prejudiced just by my sponsorship." It is the most explicit statement of the kind ever made to me, but it is a fairly common situation. I never felt that way; however, at Brown it took fifteen years to get an experimental program in which I had a deep interest adopted.

Not many hours after I had composed those words of approval for my patience in winning consent to an idea long cherished, I received a letter from an enthusiastic supporter of the innovation. His account of what happened differs so markedly from my own that it should be quoted. "I shall never forget how you first put . . . [the new courses] into effect some years ago—'foisted them on the faculty' would hardly be an overstatement. I have ever since been an admirer of that way of getting things done, and I believe, with Descartes, that a good idea is much more apt to emerge from one good mind than from a committee of them. Your first words to us that first night when the original 'group' was convoked . . . were that you wanted us to grease the skids for you, not throw up roadblocks."

Readers may wonder how two interested people on the same side of a discussion could differ so radically in their account of the origins of the same program. Partly it is due to the subtle difference of view between administrator and teacher. In this instance it is more largely because my fellow enthusiast for the new courses had not been long on the faculty and was unfamiliar with the arduous preliminary work before that final push in which he participated.

I have no illusions as to the permanence of the program at Brown. As student, teacher, and administrator I have had over fifty years of academic experience, and I am fully resigned to the cyclical aspects of educational reform. Right now there is a good deal of interest in speeding the capable preparatory student into college work, so that he enters with advanced credit. The current project was developed by the late Gordon Keith Chalmers, President of Kenyon College. It attracted the attention of great philanthropic foundations and was given a substantial subsidy. The discussions surrounding this "experiment," for the most part, assumed it was novel. Yet it was common enough fifty years ago.

I took an examination when I appeared in Middletown to enter Wesleyan, and received credit for first year German. That was not at all unusual in those days. The practice died out because, in the emphasis upon a false concept of democracy, college preparatory courses fell into decay while the stress shifted to "education for life" or "education for citizenship" or "adjustment" or some other of the successive slogans. So the rediscovery of old procedures is as novel as the voyage of Columbus, who had never heard of Eric the Red or his son Lief.

Another "novelty" of our time is accelerated graduation—some students need not take four full years to complete their baccalaureate studies. This experiment was one of the early features of the Hutchins administration at Chicago. In less highly accented manner it has been pressed as a general reform, again with foundation grants in support. But this, also, was common enough long before the current interest in the matter. Indeed, it was part of the famous Wayland reforms at Brown over a century ago. At one time during the Eliot regime, as I recall the figures, a third of each Harvard class finished in three years. I did not quite do that, but I did complete the work for both my bachelor's and master's degrees at Wesleyan in four years—though the M.A. was not conferred until a year later. Such progress was possible through independent study and writing during the summer, and passing written examinations in the fall. That method of meeting requirements made simple what is now called "acceleration." My case was by no means unique; indeed it was a common practice forty-five years ago. But like advanced credit, it fell into disfavor and dissuse.

Recently there has been a good deal of talk of individual instruction, letting the student read under guidance during the college year. It is economical, it is educational—but it is not novel. While I was a professor at Wesleyan students concentrating in history could elect up to three-fifths of their program in such informal work. Some of the best students I ever taught went to no classes; they came to my study, laid out a plan of work, and conferred from time to time on their progress.

One is tempted to say that academically "there is no new thing under the sun." But there is no occasion to be cynical about the matter. Very few ideas are like Cleopatra, of whom Enobarbus said, "Age cannot wither her, nor custom stale her infinite variety." Ideas become shopworn, they fall out of fashion, and must then be rediscovered, like the ruins of Pompeii.

Since faculties have the resistance normal to institutionalized bodies, the reformer who wants action must dress up his newly discovered (however old) idea. He must glamorize it and "sell" it if he wants to break through the crust of custom and get the faculty to change. Almost inevitably he promises too much because it takes a "hard sell" to evoke adequate response. When the reform is achieved, the salesman relaxes. The realities inevitably prove to be less than the expectations. It transpires that the enthusiasm and zeal were more important than the idea itself. Thereupon routine begins to sap the freshness of the "new" approach, and ultimately what was undertaken with such vigor succumbs to habit. This is not unique with curricular "reform," but it is certainly characteristic of it.

There is no bitterness in that remark. Education involves

endless repetition. Succeeding freshmen must be told all over again what their predecessors have been told before. The student, as student, is never carried to full maturity—but only to its threshold. Is it any wonder that staleness is so prevalent and pervasive in the academic world? It must be fought, and it can be defeated by creative research, by altering the phases of the subject with which the professor deals, by varying teaching methods, by selecting unusual students for unusual attention. However, it must also be fought institutionally by periodic reform of the curriculum. Such efforts require the faculty to reassess their patterns and procedures, to rethink their structures and requirements. And the changes are most successful when they are so radical that faculty members must really make a fresh start on at least part of their instruction.

One of the best illustrations of this process occurred at Lawrence. Victor L. Butterfield, now president at Wesleyan, developed with me a program for tutoring a small, select group of sophomores. After the custom of academics, we applied for a grant from a foundation which responded with kind words, but no funds. Nevertheless, we determined to go ahead. But before the next year opened Butterfield was offered a post at Wesleyan for double what Lawrence could pay. He suggested the appointment of Nathan M. Pusey, then studying in Greece, to carry on the project. His full duty was to give a course to thirty sophomores of unusual promise; he was to deal with them individually or in small groups, as seemed best to him. When word went round the campus that he had started these sophomores reading Aristotle's *Poetics*, the exclamations ran the gamut from dismay to amusement. To the astonishment of most, the students liked it. They were sick of textbooks. Here was something new. Instead of teaching down to them, Pusey challenged them to reach up.

The effect was electric, and not on those students alone. Professors who had been scornful of our rash expectations began to try out more difficult—better to say more substantial—reading on their students. One course for thirty sophomores could not, by itself, make much of a dent on a student body of eight hundred, each taking five courses. But as competition is the life of trade, so it is in the academic world. The sophomore tutorial was brilliantly successful in itself, but as yeast in the college it was vastly more so. It is not too much to say that this experiment was influential in raising the whole tone of instruction. The library was used not only more, but to better purpose; the quality of the books called for improved markedly, as did the number.

There was no magic in the idea of a sophomore tutorial course, and it was not essential to continue it indefinitely in that form. The value of the experiment was in demonstrating—so that an entire academic community must see it—that the level of their expectations had been too low. There is a phrase now current to describe the situation in what are called "underdeveloped countries"—a "revolution of rising expectations." The academic world, during the last half century, has seen a devolution of diminished expectations. I have long been convinced that the greatest educational error of our time has been an underestimation of the students. They react favorably to better standards every time; they take pride in doing work worthy of their best effort. The "Gentleman's C" has been a curse, not only on those who got it, but even more on those who gave it; it served to reduce scholastic performance to an unwarranted degree.

At Brown the courses in the identification and criticism of ideas have been, like the sophomore tutorial at Lawrence, more important as yeast than as bread. Some of them, many I think, have been brilliantly successful. But as a stimulus to competition they have been superb. Academic rote tends to be a treadmill; if it suddenly appears that a colleague is not just going round and round but is actually trying to get somewhere—and getting there—the effort is contagious.

A president cannot "boss" a faculty these days. It is rare indeed when he can lead it. But he can stimulate it, and he should. Such activity will not make him the benign or the well-beloved; but the object of holding office is educational progress, not popularity.

In all he says and does the president must avoid even the appearance of favoritism. Personal preferences there are certain to be. Friendships will be formed—and antipathies. Such relationships must be regarded as irrelevant to official actions. In such matters the president should divorce his feelings from his performances just as a surgeon must operate with as much emotional detachment as is humanly possible.

Finally, in administering the faculty the president must not lose his sense of humor. There will always be rebels who will fight whatever he does. There will always be "liberals" in politics who prove to be hard-shell conservatives in matters academic. There will be the dogmatists who resent his failure to worship their particular golden calf. There will be those who needle him, as a matter of principle, because there should be no such thing as an "administration" in a society of scholars. These slings and arrows are not outrageous fortune, they are the common hazards of his office. Once that lesson is learned a president can bear them not so much with fortitude as with laughter. He can smile at the rebels and the rock-ribbed liberals outside and equally rock-ribbed conservatives inside the institution; he can shrug off the dogmatists and needlers. Furthermore he should save some of his laughter for himself, because no man is deft enough to do all a president is obligated to attempt without being ludicrous from time to time.

IV

The Administration

ADMINISTRATION of a college or university is directly conditioned by two factors. Both are exceedingly simple in nature; neither gets as much attentive thought as it deserves.

First: colleges have no "product" at all; they exist to develop people. They manufacture no widgets or gadgets or mechanical items which can be standardized, mass produced, counted, weighed, measured, and accepted as perfect or rejected as defective. People are remarkable in that we know relatively so little about them despite the vastness of our knowledge. We deliberately and properly make our problem the more insoluble by commitment to the democratic philosophy. When we seek, consciously and energetically, to develop every individual to his fullest capacity, we are making any but the crudest classification almost impossible. Precise measurement becomes absolutely impossible.

A favorite quotation with me comes from Thomas Mann who spoke of education as an "optimistic and humane" enterprise. The optimism is vital. When we graduate a person we do not know what he will become. The Phi Beta Kappa student may become a Bowery bum; one of my friends did. The last time I saw him he burst into the University Club in New York to cadge enough money for drink and dope. He had once been an able scholar and an attractive man. At the other extreme the boy who just scrapes through may become touched with ambition and achieve a brilliant career.

Statistically, of course, we can make some reasonably accurate predictions. But in the education of an individual statistics give a range of probabilities, no certainties. It follows that alleged measurements of the quality of the education supplied at a given institution are an estimate, a judgment, a guess—frequently influenced by a loyal prejudice or a hostile bias. When someone publishes a list of the ten best universities or the ten best colleges it is an instance of a man talking through his hat.

These things being so, the administrator who concentrates on the external evidences of success in education may attain a reputation which has little relationship to the realities. The central business of a president is to do everything he can, and facilitate everything anyone else can do, to stretch individual students to their full capacity, to stimulate them to independence in thought, word, and deed. Independence is not manifested by growing a beard when others are clean shaven, or wearing odd clothes, or joining a picket line in which, as an individual, he has no stake. Such externals may mean much or little. The genuine task is the cultivation of a mind that seeks to express itself in its own way at its own best level.

With the possible exception of the church, which has a specialized part in this process, institutions of higher education occupy a unique place in the scheme of things in that they graduate individual people—no two alike. Since commercial operations cannot produce people, general comparisons with businesses which have wholly different objectives are more likely to be confusing than revealing.

The second fundamental factor which should shape the administrative effort also has to do with persons. The apparatus by which the college's ends are achieved is composed of people. There is no such thing as machine-made education. In this respect, also, educational institutions share with the church a unique position in the scheme of things. Automation is not possible; many of the economies of mass production are totally irrelevant; indeed they may well be dangerous.

What is this organization of people, working on other people their juniors in age, learning, and experience, trying to do? If they are attempting merely to pass on the knowledge accumulated in the past, and to a limited extent they are, some of the semiautomatic or apparently automatic methods of putting stuff in cans have a modicum of relevance. It seems extraordinary, however, that the exponents of mass media in education are so vigorous in their insistence upon the human voice, as though students had not learned to read or the book been invented. The lecture is the slowest and least effective mode for the transmission of knowledge. It became the norm before books were widely and inexpensively available. As a means of transmitting facts it is obsolete. Yet that is the method most often promoted by the enthusiasts for "stuffing the students" with data.

The human contact is most effective in developing the individual student if it is provocative and evocative, not just vocal. If a student cannot read, or if he does not, his education in a meaningful sense is meager, impoverished; in any event it stops when he leaves college. He may hear news on the radio and commentary; he may listen to an occasional lecture. But if he has become acclimated to learning from the human voice, and primarily through his ears, his commencement, of which the orators so often speak in June, is the beginning of a decline in intellectual interest, activity, and growth. After graduation he is virtually cut off from the source of supply he has come to regard as normal.

College is a place and an instrument to promote human

growth by the human effort of teacher and taught. If it is not that, it is not worthy to be called college. This sounds exceedingly simple; but it is a hard gospel indeed, and the administrator had best recognize that fact at the start. Early realization will both limit and expand his activity. It will show him that many of the gestures so common to college administration are futile. If he puts time and energy upon unessentials his work will quickly lose freshness and he will soon be bored. And boredom is the bane of administration. Routines there are, and we cannot live without them; but when we come to live by them, zest evaporates rapidly and boredom moves in. I have known more presidents to suffer from that administrative disease than any other. So far as effectiveness in the educative process is concerned, it is fatal.

But a proper concept of education in college expands the interest and activity of the president and makes boredom incredible. He will realize as fundamental that the classroom is only one of the places where the educative process takes place, and it is by no means always the most important. If college administration is to be educationally effective every conceivable environmental stimulus to the growth of the student must be developed. Beyond all else he must be encouraged to do more and more things for himself and by himself. The title of a recent best seller—on another topic—carries the root idea: *How to Do Nothing with Nobody All Alone by Yourself*.

Since an academic tradition stronger than law forbids the president to invade the classroom or tamper directly with instruction, his most rewarding educational efforts will be in environmental and instrumental areas. There he can exert an indirect influence far more potent than any "interference" could achieve.

The library, for example, can reflect his educational philosophy. I learned about the way students use—or fail to use

—the library in my earliest days at Wesleyan, when I had to "serve time" as assistant reference librarian with no principal reference librarian to guide or instruct me. I discovered at that early stage of my career that the reserve shelf, instead of facilitating use of books, was often, in actual practice, a barrier to their effective employment. Many students never touched any other books; the catalogue, the reference works, bibliographical aides of every kind were all neglected.

From first-hand contact I found out that the contents of the reserve shelf supplied a fairly accurate index of diminishing expectations on the part of the professor, and concrete evidence that the student was being short-changed in his education. The professors who were most successful induced students to buy books as well as to read widely from the library collections. They required writing which involved bibliographical work. Their list of reserved books was short or nonexistent. I could learn more about a professor's teaching effectiveness by observing the use his students made of the library than by studying the poll conducted by the student paper or by listening to undergraduate gossip. The knowledge acquired through my library experience profoundly influenced my administrative philosophy and course of action.

At Lawrence the library had traditionally been a respository. The books were kept—and pretty effectively kept away from students. The stacks were "closed"; various routines in taking a book out of the building set up formidable obstacles. The reserve shelf *was* the library so far as most students were concerned. One department, I discovered, did not order a book to be bought for the library during three entire semesters; and no member of the faculty in that department took a book from the library in the same period. So striking an instance of poor instruction startled me, and I wondered how common was such neglect of the library resources. Consequently I sought light on the practice of other faculty members.

Thereupon I joined with the librarian in a long and rather complex study of the books borrowed by faculty members, both in quantity and quality, as well as the number and kind of books they purchased for their own and for student use. After what seemed like a mountain of figures had been gathered, a good deal of effort was put into analyzing them and classifying the faculty into four groups. The broad assumption was that the best teachers and scholars make the fullest and most varied use of the library and stimulate their students to do likewise.

When all that had been done, I asked the members of the faculty who had "tenure" to rate each other—anonymously—into four groups. I then compared the two lists—the one based on statistical evidence drawn from the use of the library, the other on the judgment of the teachers' peers. The similarity between the two sets of estimates—one "objective," the other "subjective"—was startling. For a number of reasons I never made that procedure into a regular technique. Nevertheless it had a marked effect on my administration. Every president who has any sensitivity at all is worried lest personal feelings and individual bias warp his professional estimates. This study gave me some assurance that I was learning to form judgments as objectively—as professionally—as is humanly possible.

In subsequent years I never again had an opportunity to gather similar detailed statistical evidence. It was possible in a small college; in a university the conditions and problems are so complex that any such relatively simple method would be valueless. Furthermore the general judgment of all a man's colleagues would not be so reliable in the larger society, where specialization has gone very much further, and in a larger community, where intimate contacts are rarer and more restricted.

At the same time that the study of the faculty was in progress, we sought to learn how many different books were actually used in the course of a year in libraries of colleges with good reputations. One of the first discoveries was that most statistics were not helpful; they were not even meaningful. The reason was simple: they did not measure the same things in different institutions, and were therefore not comparable. For example, one famous college in the East made it a practice to order many copies of textbooks—sometimes as many as 150. It also had multiple copies of the "principal" reserve books. Every student who read his assignment of eight or ten pages was credited with using a book; statistics soared, while effective reading stagnated. In another college, which refused to have multiple copies of texts and required students to buy them, the library circulation appeared to be much less, whereas the use of its resources was actually much greater. In short, the statistics kept in college libraries required so much interpretation that most raw figures were worthless.

Among colleges that boasted of the size of their libraries, few could give the inquirer any close approximation of the proportion of their collections which were ever touched by students or faculty. When the figure was available it was often astoundingly small. In one instance not over 4,000 different books were taken from the shelves in a college of 1,000 students and a library of a quarter of a million volumes. In consideration of the fact that nearly 1,500 of the volumes were on reserve, the sterility of the balance, so far as use was concerned, was obvious. It proved that there was little independent reading and not much serious written work requiring bibliographical search and the use of multiple sources. It showed that instruction was vocal, that reading was primarily in textbooks, that initiative was not being stimulated or developed, that the learning process was inadequately creative.

Naturally, having been a scholar, I did not regard all seldom-used books as deadwood. Wesleyan had bought a whole set of somewhat rare books for my research use. They got heavy employment by me for ten years. In that time only one or two other persons consulted them; in the next decade they may have been untouched until some other faculty research project brought them again into active demand. Making every allowance for research material I found the narrowly restricted range of use of library resources shocking.

The library is in many respects the very heart of the college. It ought, therefore, to be a major preoccupation of its principal administrative officer. At Lawrence I made drastic changes. In appointing a new librarian I selected a woman trained and experienced in public libraries. Because she did not pretend to be a scholar, I took over direction of the books to be bought, working closely with the various departments of instruction. The librarian was a first-class organizer and insisted that the catalogue, which was not uniform but followed various systems for various periods of acquistion, must be remade. Working together we got some money, brought in a specialist, and recatalogued the entire collection, making it much more usable. We set up a reference department, theretofore nonexistent, and watched it grow. The acceleration in its employment suggested clearly the advance in the educational process. Every effort was made to stimulate recreational reading and to interest students in books outside their courses. To that end we resorted to a whole series of devices.

The books put on the "reserve shelf" were studied with extreme care. It became manifest, after long scrutiny, that more than a quarter were never called for at all. Another fifty percent were used five times or less during an entire year. The bulk of the use was concentrated in less than a quarter of the whole number. Moreover the active service of a "reserve book" usually occupied a relatively short time. Thus even those volumes which were "statistically active" were idle most of the months they were kept on reserve. This led to an astonishing discovery: many books actually circulated more often when not on reserve—a fact which astounded professors who had assumed the contrary to be true. Subsequently I tested that conclusion again and again, and always with the same result.

For thirty years, therefore, I waged war on the reserve shelf—not to abolish it completely, but to keep it in scale and reduce its adverse effect upon the broader use of the library. The campaign had various degrees of success and failure. But if I were to begin all over again I should fight even harder. In "real life," as the commencement orators so often refer to the years after graduation, there is no reserve shelf. If we seek to make students into intellectual self-starters, we should inculcate, during college, the habits which will be useful thereafter.

This warfare illustrates one point about administration that is not often mentioned. The board of trustees, the faculty, and the president can adopt a policy, announce it—even proclaim it. But the real policy is not what they say, but what is done, often by an officer with no policy-making authority at all. Two or three years before I retired from Brown a new instructor came in to make a courtesy call. He had been abroad when appointed, so this was our first meeting. He was a graduate of a college in whose library I had seen row upon row of duplicate copies of textbooks; there was one well known—but now somewhat dated—economic text with no less than fifty copies each of several successive editions.

After the usual civilities I inquired how he was planning his work. Thereupon he entered enthusiastically into a description of his first enterprise—assembling the largest collection of reserved books in the appropriate reading room. After listening politely as long as I could stand it, I startled him by commenting, "I want to congratulate you. During your first forty-eight hours on the campus you have reversed a policy upon which I have been working for fifteen years."

The episode highlights an aspect of the presidency as a "political" office. The president has no power to command a member of the faculty. He can seek to influence him by persuasion, but any officer of instruction is free to go his own way and pursue his own policy touching instruction. I could, and did, criticize textbooks as desiccated summaries, predigested pabulum—using any opprobrious term that seemed to me appropriate. I could endorse the use of more substantial and rewarding reading, and adduce evidence that not only would the students read the classics, but would prefer them to texts and actually enjoy them. However, if the professor was wedded to his idols, there was no academic heresy in his addiction. He remained the master of his own instruction and, subject to a minimum number of faculty regulations, could pursue his own policy.

In the administrative phases of the library, however, the president has much more scope. The librarian as bibliographer, as professor, has the same independence as any other officer of instruction, but as administrator he is subject to policy direction. We found at Lawrence, for example, that a hospitable attitude at the delivery desk had a marked influence. When I reached Brown the delivery desk was a cage, protected by heavy wire. The books were given out through an opening smaller than used to be found in an old-fashioned bank teller's cage. An enlargement of the library building furnished the opportunity to get rid of that and install an open counter. The students quickly had a name for it, "Hank's bar, the longest in town."

If a president exerts enough pressure, he can pry open the stack entrance so that books may be seen, touched—and conceivably read. While at Lawrence I worked with a laboratory furniture company and designed carrels for installation in the stacks so that students could write essays close to the books they wanted to use. At Brown access to the full collection was facilitated and as many carrels as possible installed. A "students' library"—virtually an enlarged reserve shelf—was discontinued.

One of the things which impressed me about college library "reading rooms" was their gregarious atmosphere. While I was at Wesleyan we had no reading room to speak of; there was no space for it. Lawrence gave me my first experience with such an institution. In the early days there it often seemed to me that the library was used more for dating than for reading. Who first designed reading rooms as imitations of the Grand Central Terminal I do not know; magnificent as that concourse is, it is no place to read. At Brown the big reading room was broken up into three smaller ones; three other reading rooms were constructed or reconstructed. The atmosphere was altered from that of a highly disciplined hall to a more relaxed environment—to which better furnishings contributed.

However, if students are going to develop good reading habits they should be encouraged, so far as possible, to take books to their own rooms. In that enterprise we had conspicuous success at Lawrence. Attainment of this goal made enlargement of the reading room unnecessary. It prevented leaving vast cubage idle large portions of the time—and overcrowded briefly just before examinations.

In setting up listening rooms for poetry reading or for music, in establishing a library of pictures to be circulated like books, and in dozens of other ways a president can give administrative leadership in making the library function more educationally. This also illustrates a fundamental administrative technique: the president must not be—or seek to become—the librarian. He should work with the head of the library in creating an atmosphere, in developing ways and means of student access and service. In sum, he should set policy, not from his office, by memo, or by fiat, but through intimate and frequent contact with the operation until he understands the particular problems which must be met. Once policy is set—not in words alone, but in action—he need no longer give so much time to the library, but can turn his attention elsewhere, leaving the librarian to carry the load, save when he requires occasional help which the president must stand ready to supply.

It is astonishing what progress can be made by actively promoting the free and full use of books by students. But that end will not be achieved by some dramatic—not to say gaudy—"plan." The use of the library grew so rapidly at Lawrence that it attracted attention, and after a few years of steady advance I was asked to write an article giving the recipe. There was no single answer. I, myself, was astonished by the realization that the change, however notable, was the result of a great many relatively small adjustments of policy. Not all occurred in the library itself. Alteration in teaching methods and emphasis by a large share of the faculty, stress on written work, reduction of dependence upon textbooks—these and many other factors had a cumulative effect. Administration does not consist in following a "system," but in dealing continuously and flexibly—and persistently—with situations as they arise.

Another major barrier to the fulfillment of the highest goals of education has been student living conditions. The most famous president in Brown's history, Francis Wayland, made the point clear over a century ago: "We assume the responsibility of a superintendence which we have rendered ourselves incapable of fulfilling; . . . we have lost the humanizing effect produced by daily association of students with older and well-bred gentlemen, so obvious in an English college; . . . we have expended almost all the funds appropriated to education in the construction of unsightly buildings, we had almost said barracks, for which, perhaps, the highest merit that can be claimed is, that they are not positively and universally a nuisance." He was elaborating upon what should be a truism that a residential college loses much of its character if student accommodations approximate army quarters rather than residences.

In my college days at Wesleyan I lived in a mansion. The only dormitory had burned some time before I matriculated; the replacement was not ready. The fraternity house where I resided belonged to the Alsop family. It was set in beautiful grounds, well planted, and the freshmen had to maintain the gardens. The living rooms downstairs were frescoed by artists brought over from Italy, and whenever a roughhouse began the cry of "frescoes" brought speedy order. There was statuary, painted and of marble. The sleeping accommodations approximated barracks, but the living rooms and studies had spaciousness and even elegance.

The building was of such a character as to invite respect —and get it. The rules were such that a student who wished to study could do so without serious annoyance. When a man closed his door it meant he wanted privacy—not interruption. The housemother was a maiden lady of great dignity to whose Victorian whims we deferred rather amazingly. Those in residence were not plaster saints, but there was an internal and domestic discipline which was healthy. The house, its setting, its appointments, its atmosphere were all one could hope for in a student residence.

During my teaching years, except as I served as adviser to my fraternity chapter, I had little contact with dormitories and their management. When I arrived at Lawrence, I received a shock. As noted earlier, the men's dormitory had been badly damaged by fire the June before my September arrival. The repairs completed during the summer were hasty, not of the best workmanship, and did nothing to make the building livable. The furniture in the "living room" was designed to resist abuse—but was ugly enough to provoke it. The floor was bare, the walls were bleak, the paint neutral, a sort of "landlord's buff"—"so as not to show dirt."

The atmosphere was bad. A professor lived in the building and ruled it like a prison. There was a fine of twenty-five cents if an electric light was left on during dinner. Each room was limited to a minimum wattage; no "electrical appliances" were permitted. Fines were levied for a whole series of "offenses"—which they stimulated. The food was under the supervision of an untrained—and not well-experienced—woman. The students insisted that they were served "barrel gravy" and there was only a small margin of error in the complaint. In fact, that dormitory seemed to me worse than those Wayland had denounced in 1850—for it was, from my point of view, "positively and universally a nuisance."

In a somewhat different sense the women's dormitories were as bad. There was the same limitation on adequate lighting; it would be better to say the same insistence upon inadequate lighting. The two principal dormitories were sharply differentiated in character, appointments, and in social standing. One was "new," its furniture reasonably well chosen; it had an elevator (of sorts and of moods); most of the sorority members lived in it. The other was "old," dingy, rundown; its furniture was largely inherited; the tables in the dining room were the "gifts" of Appleton families that wanted up-to-date appointments; the dining chairs, similarly, were a miscellaneous collection of castoffs. The kitchen and its equipment were antiquated. Everything combined to give occupants the feeling of being second-class citizens—and they were so regarded.

What I found on that campus was no exception. If it had been it would not be worth mentioning. As I went about among colleges I discovered conditions in Lawrence dormitories were more nearly typical than otherwise. During a spring recess a meeting of Midwest college presidents was held at one of the best, and most famous, of the colleges. We were housed in a brand-new dormitory, being occupied for the first year. It was sound in construction, but no care had been given the amenities, and there had been no consideration for the value of silence. I could hear every move in the rooms on either side, and the one above. As an experiment I asked one of my confreres to drop a pin—without notice and casually. He did—and it was perfectly audible to me. The furniture was solid, of poor design, and uncomfortable. The beds were hard and narrow, with thin mattresses. No picture moldings were provided and there were strong prohibitions against nails, tacks—or glue—to hang pictures. New as it was, electric outlets were few, wiring was skimpy, and wattage closely rationed.

During this era business officers selected a term to use for dormitories and dining rooms in their accounting procedure; they were called "auxiliary enterprises." The phrase annoyed me when I first heard it; it is still in use, and I still find it irksome. This irritation does not grow out of some semantic preference on my part. The objection arises from the philosophy of education which the term accurately reflects. It makes explicit a failure to appreciate that living conditions are an integral element in education, not a sideline.

Much less should residences and dining halls constitute a

profit-making sideline. At Lawrence I found that alleged "profits" from housing and feeding were being used to meet direct "educational" costs. Actually there were no real profits. The cash balances, mislabeled "profits," which appeared regularly in the treasurer's books, and were "transferred" to instructional costs, were a fairly accurate measure of the deterioration of the buildings—a failure of maintenance. As the "capitalization" of library books and other current expenses was consistently robbing the endowment, these alleged "profits" were with equal consistency dissipating plant assets. Usually dormitories stay in use a century or more. Too few are built with any such length of service in mind; fewer still are maintained with that period of utility in mind. It became a fundamental article of faith with me that maintenance of the quality of living conditions and of food was of the first importance—educationally as well as fiscally.

Any other program shows that the lesson Wayland sought to teach over a century ago, the lesson the British colleges absorbed long since, is still not learned in America. If one were deliberately to set out to separate the liberal ideal from reality, by putting it in an inappropriate environment, it would be difficult to imagine how more effectively to accomplish the project. The quadrangles at Chicago, the "houses" at Harvard, the "colleges" at Yale were all attempts to make learning and living part of an integral process. They were designed as residences. Time has, to some extent, eroded the ideal; some of the handsome dining rooms have come to be operated more as mess halls than anything appropriate to a college. I was deeply shocked at the contrast between my first visit in a high-paneled dining hall, where I had an interesting, well-served meal, and my last experience in the same hall—self-service on an army-type tray from a steam-table inappropriately set in the midst of the structural elegance.

The difference in the tone of student behavior during the meal was as notable as the alteration in atmosphere; indeed, it directly reflected it.

Insistence upon the point of view that living and learning should be part of the same process can come only from the president—there is no other source from which it can stem. It is not an easy assignment for him to fulfill. Built-in habits of consulting the balance sheet instead of reviewing educational philosophy are hard to alter, and when those habits *appear* to help support the narrowly defined "educational" budget they are especially tough in their resistance to change. As a result it must be by persistent evolution that improvement is wrought—unless some Harkness comes along to make it dramatic to the point of being revolutionary.

At Lawrence I began by changing the faculty resident from the status of warden of a prison to that of counselor. Discipline he had to handle to some extent, but that was primarily the dean's business. The resident was supposed to live the life of a gentleman and a scholar, as an example, a leader. Ideal candidates for such posts are rare, and when found are not always available. But if the appointee is chosen with the same careful consideration that is used in filling an important faculty post, progress can result. However, it is a point at which administrative fatigue is likely to set in very early. The first appointment is made with thoughtful care, because reform is the goal. When conditions are improved a replacement is likely to be named with less study. Then the situation can deteriorate by slow degrees—almost imperceptibly, until sudden collapse reveals the fatal character of the process. The fight for good dormitory leadership is perpetual. Permanent victory is as elusive as permanent peace; defeat is always close at hand.

The second step in dormitory reform was physical. I have not counted the number of kitchens I have participated in building or rebuilding. Recently I went back to inspect one, now many years old. It was as good as new; it was an instance where I had resisted every plea to "economize"—at the expense of the quality of the installation. At no other point in the whole college does apparent extravagance pay such large dividends. Poor food means poor morale in students at their "eatingest" age; poison food—one of the greatest of all hazards in feeding large numbers—infuriates parents as well as students. No one can hope to satiate the appetites of freshmen and sophomores; no one can satisfy their whims or even their prejudices. As one brilliant faculty member expressed it, "They prefer incredible edibles to comely comestibles." But it is possible to make a heroic effort—and it must be continuous. In this, too, victory is transient, defeat endemic.

Similarly the living rooms and lounges require thought. When I reached Brown no men's dormitory had any sort of common room or lounge. I was told it "had been tried"; it had, indeed, but feebly and without much faith. The key to success in this matter is to make the commons such a room as demands respect. One who travels constantly soon learns that a quick and reliable test of the difference between a good hotel and a poor one is the lounge furniture. Plastic where fabric should be, solidity without grace, ugliness instead of beauty—these show the poor taste, the meager expectations of the management. It is so with dormitories: the broad rule is that students will accord the same respect to furniture that the college does. Poor furniture will get poor treatment. Of course good furniture will too—occasionally. This is true even in the home. But as false economy in instruction cheats the students, so also does underestimating their capacity to appreciate good line, good fabric, good decoration.

The student's own room should reflect his growth—his education. When I went to college my room had banners, and some pictures. Both were highly unsophisticated. I had been in a museum only once or twice in my life. I had lived in parsonages with things chosen by committees; their selections were usually the epitome of poor taste—and badly worn. In moments of reverie I can still smell the horsehair which covered sofa and chairs because it was "durable"; it was, desperately so. There was no course in art in college—art was not once mentioned in my four years so far as I can remember. When, therefore, I chose a "hand-colored" photograph by Wallace Nutting it was decorative—but naive to a degree.

When I took office as president and saw what adorned students' walls in dormitories there was no occasion for surprise, but much need for action. Under the inspiration and guidance of my wife, art exhibits were begun; then a collection of framed pictures was bought, to be rented to students. The rental charge was the same for the very few originals as for the reproductions of etchings taken from books. The object was to induce the students to choose for values other than financial, to develop their taste by living with pictures. And the gains they made in the sophistication of their choices between the freshman and senior year were proof enough that this was education, not mere decoration.

In one ambition I was frustrated for the entire thirty years of my terms of office. I felt that students should have a wider choice in setting their own residential tone than is ordinarily possible with uniform beds, standard chests, identical desks, chairs, mirrors. Some men would like to have rooms like offices, others like living rooms. That was possible for me and my fellow students at Wesleyan. To achieve the full result for a whole college would require a furniture warehouse and some good sample rooms—and I never found enough money. Yet I believe that it was a sound idea educationally.

One of the tragedies of the new "economy" dormitories often built with government loans is that they are narrowing, rather than broadening, the student's opportunity to express —and to develop—his own taste. Before the quadrangles at Brown were built I went about to study what was being done elsewhere. In one state university the cubage per student was at the absolute legal minimum. The furniture was all built in; the student could not rearrange his room even to the smallest degree. The dormitory director told me explicitly that it was forbidden to put pictures of any sort on the walls by any method; I asked the dean if this could be true and he confirmed the report. The dormitory was new, strong, sterile —and antieducational. It will stand for a century as a monument to bad taste, bad educational philosophy—and people will weep at the tastelessness of graduates from such an environment. Not all the "instruction" in art will prevail over living experience.

Another of my own undergraduate episodes led to a further change in dormitory practice. In the garret where we all had bunks, each boy took care of his bed. Some were careful and even meticulous, but one lad slept between the same sheets a whole semester. The seniors finally made an issue of it and he grudgingly conformed to minimum requirements. The memory of this made me a missionary for clean sheets.

Even with the absurd hours students keep, they manage to spend a good many hours in bed. So at Lawrence year by year every old bed was replaced by a new one; linen was furnished—and changed—regularly. When students went to the gymnasium, they had clean clothes each time. Physical education should not proceed in filth. Stress upon the style of living is as vital as any other part of an education.

The final change in dormitory matters was professional management. Running a residential system with cleanliness, order, and economy, with an eye to student comfort and growth, requires sound training and experience. Nowhere else about the institution is there greater need for professional skill. Its cost may appear to be high, but the dividends upon the investment are even higher.

As with the library, getting policy and procedure established is an engrossing task. Once the tone is set, once the staff has organized efficiently, once the essential physical changes have been accomplished, the president can turn his attention to other matters, with, however, occasional inspection and reappraisal. In no other phase of college administration is eternal vigilance more essential.

Buildings and grounds constitute yet another basic responsibility of a president. No one else can have any deep concern for the total effect; if he is not profoundly concerned, no one else is likely to be. For there is no other center of responsibility. The faculty is not accountable, nor are the deans. Only seldom are business officers ready to leave their desks and roam around; of all college officers they seem to me the most completely sedentary—desk-bound. I was fortunate enough to work with men who were ambulatory, but such are rare. So much are buildings and grounds the concern of the president that one can tell a lot about the kind of officer he is by looking at the grass on the campus—is it healthy, cut, smooth?

When I went to Lawrence its campus in the heart of the city was ragged. The new business manager came from a state agricultural college; he told me the trees were too closely spaced, were not well formed, and would get worse, not better, with time. I was ignorant about such matters, and skeptical. Nonetheless, I let him cut down a few—and survived the uproar which was considerable. Before many years he was proved right. The trees grew more gracefully, the lawns were better. The campus became a center of beauty. New, well-drained walks dried quickly after rain, and made snow clearance by machine easy. Most people see no connection between sidewalks and student health, but well-drained walkways reduce the number of wet feet and consequent infirmary calls.

After I transferred to Brown a comprehensive campus program had to be undertaken. A volunteer with a genius for landscaping assumed the task, making laurel, dogwood, magnolia brighten the spring; a wide variety of planting was accomplished, and grass was cultivated. After a time my function was reduced to insistence on budget appropriations and backing the volunteer against the passive resistance of the maintenance staff and the accounting whims of the controller. The atmospheric change which concern for layout, for color and variety, for sweeping away cigarette stubs will produce is incalculable. Education proceeds best—as at Oxford—where gardens are integral to the scheme of things.

The president can well spend some time surveying buildings. My experience at Lawrence on the occasion of my visit to be "looked over" taught me a lesson. I never wanted a "guided tour"; instead I would start at the basement and work through to the attic—with note and comment. It is astonishing what can be achieved by such detailed inspections. In one laboratory building there were no less than three centrifuges on floors in different places; they were "broke," said the janitor, "no good," said the chairman. A new chairman got them off the floor, repaired, and five years later all were still in constant use. One "crowded" laboratory building had twenty percent of its space devoted to storage of things never used; when the junk was sorted, sold, or dumped, maintenance was less, occupancy was notably increased—and the safety and value of the building enhanced. The cost of that restored cubage, if it had been replaced by new construction, would have been over two hundred thousand dollars.

When the superintendent of buildings, the janitors, the groundsmen, the plumbers, electricians, carpenters, painters all know that the president is interested, perhaps knowledgeable, and certainly ubiquitous, the effect is tangible.

The library, the residences, the grounds illustrate a central point. Nothing that touches the life of faculty or student should be alien to the interest and thought of the president. The lawns, the trees, tennis courts, swimming pool—these and hundreds of other details—must come under his occasional surveillance. The mere setting down of that sentence makes it transparently clear that he cannot supervise all such things all the time. There are not hours enough in the day nor energy enough in any man to do all he must do if he tries to do it all at once and all himself. Moreover, if he concentrates too long on one area of interest, it will become routine and precipitate boredom—earlier described as the greatest enemy of sound administration.

What I have just written seems at first to justify a passage in a weekly news magazine commenting upon the appointment of a new chancellor at the Berkeley campus of the University of California: ". . . many scientists will . . . wonder whether one of the world's best chemists should pour himself into the world of university management—which, even at one of the best campuses in the nation, consists largely of parking problems, building plans and ruffled regents." But that is the superficial view of a journalist with more concern for a slick sentence than perceptive accuracy. The business of the president is to create a sound environment, the right atmosphere, physical as well as intellectual, for the educative process. As good housekeeping contributes to a good home, so good administration facilitates good education. If such duties are not always glamorous, neither are all aspects of any other career—even science, which has arid stretches of deadly routine. If the administrator's duties do not appear to be central to the great issues, they are no less essential. And if the president manages these matters well, he can be free to put his energies into other areas which appear to be—though they are not always—more vital.

Only by building a capable staff and inculcating his ideas into their work can a president even oversee all he must do. If he is a real professional and is making educational administration his life work, he has not only a right but an obligation to shape the administrative staff and mold their duties. He is the chosen instrument of the board of trustees, he has the responsibility for dominating administration. There is no academic freedom for administrators. They have no such formal tenure as professors, though they may acquire what almost amounts to it in time.

In most circumstances it takes from four to five years for a new president to become master in his own house. There are holdovers from the previous administration: they may be wedded to its ways. At Lawrence the alumni secretary calmly told me that he was going to continue to follow the orders of my predecessor, and would not be bound by any directions from me. It was an extreme—and explicit—instance of what is far too common—pursuing old habits that reflect a different spirit and sometimes a different direction. The alumni secretary was stubborn, but he had no tenure, and shortly no job. However, the dean was there, and many circumstances made a change inadvisable—even if I had known then how to effect it. As I said in an earlier chapter, the bulk of his work was done by me and by young people "over his head," so to speak, until he reached retirement age.

Developing his own team constitutes no adverse judgment of the previous administration. The group surrounding the president must fit his rhythm. That does not mean that they are "yes men"; I never had any of those about me, nor wanted any; the office is already too isolated; "yes men" remove it further from vital contacts. Nor does it mean that the president's appointees are, or should be, cronies. Often—

though by no means always—my intimate friends were outside the range of my closest administrative associates. It means simply that, without favoritism or personal appeal, the president chooses men and women—on as detached and objective a basis as is humanly possible—who can do the regular and necessary daily chores as well as cooperate with him on new programs and fresh adventures.

Both at Lawrence and at Brown I was fortunate in finding professional business managers who had minds of their own and were articulate in expressing them, yet were willing to follow broad policies for which I was responsible. Similarly, in both instances, we located first-class professionals to manage dormitories and dining rooms, men and women who saw those tasks in educational terms.

The relationship of the president with his immediate associates is not a major problem. With the provost, the business manager, vice presidents, and the deans he can get along fairly easily. He sees them often enough to be influenced by them and to influence them. As in almost all human relations there will be differences of opinion, which occasionally produce friction and heat. Those episodes are rare and, in a healthy institution, soon forgotten. The principal difficulty, in my experience, has been with the second line—the men and women not responsible directly to the president, but to him through another.

Two of these I came to think of as "the enemy." That appellation had nothing whatever to do with the men personally; indeed my personal relations were often cordial, even warm. But the registrar and the controller were often in my hair and they had some share in its early disappearance. The reason can be stated in very few words. Those two jobs approach more closely the innately bureaucratic than any others in a whole university. They involve following routines, and acting by votes, by rules and regulations, by "standards." These officers are, for the most part, separated from direct contact with human problems; their material is figures, statistical data. Of course those are necessary, but they are subsidiary even though essential.

When the registrar makes his calculations he is affecting a human life—but not directly, therefore not with human sensibility. Too often when the student comes to him with a personal problem he gets a quoted rule for an answer. Too often when he wants help he gets an average for a reply. In a sense, this is the nature of the registrar's job. The only alleviation I ever found was to isolate the statistician from the students as much as possible and make their contacts with the deans; deans, almost by definition, deal with human situations, and do it humanly—or "resign."

What the registrar does to the students, the controller is likely to do to the faculty. He assigns a charge for goods or services to some "account" bearing a cabalistic number. The range of his free authority in this matter is relatively narrow but its exercise can be irritating to a degree. Every person who calls for an expenditure would prefer to have it charged to someone else. A laboratory sink is clogged; "buildings and grounds" fixes it. To the instructional department this is a normal maintenance cost of buildings and grounds and chargeable to the superintendent's budget. But to that organization it is a departmental cost for laboratory operation.

The controller will infuriate the professor if the charge is against his budget; he will enrage the superintendent if it is put against maintenance. His decision is apt to be a legalistic one that makes no sense to either party and irritates both. Sometimes it seems to me that in thirty years of dealing with faculties many of the most acute emotional scenes arose from accounting procedures that were "stupid," "unfair," "outrageous," and so on and so forth. The aggrieved faculty member could "prove" that the cost of opening a clogged drain, when charged to his budget, was several times the charge when it was assigned to buildings and grounds.

The heat was often transferred to other quarters. The business manager tended to support his subordinates, the superintendent and the controller; the dean was a partisan of his colleague, the professor. And the president was between the upper and the nether millstones. Yet, from his point of view—a view apparently unique with him—it was the college's money which was involved, not the resources of either of the disputants.

This sort of disagreement is fresh illustration of the fact that very few administrative troubles grow out of matters of real substance. When something genuinely important is involved all concerned make an effort to take a sane, long-range view. It is when the issues are essentially trivial—the cost of a clogged drain—that restraints are thrown off and donnybrook supervenes. All too often the prime movers in these irritations are the controller and the registrar. I came to accept the offices as necessary evils—often held by very fine men whose personal charm was equaled only by their official prickliness.

The fundamental reason for these difficulties lies, I believe, in the inelasticity of the jobs themselves. They call for many different activities and skills, but, once those are mastered, they do not offer so much variety and change of pace as other college tasks.

As for other officers—in policy-making posts particularly—appointing good people is only half the battle—or even less. Keeping them interested and refreshing their viewpoints are just as important. I believe the key to that is the same as with the president himself. They must be provided with variety in their work, lest routine sap all the liveliness from their tasks. Administration calls for endless repetition—but not necessarily by the same person all the time. For this reason I developed a theory of administration which I cannot claim was ever popular; indeed my associates sometimes complained of it rather bitterly. However, it was based on conviction and experience.

To state it is simple: I never had a chart of organization or a set of sharply prescribed duties. If an officer worked out such a scheme it was subject to change—on short notice. On one occasion at Brown I asked two vice presidents virtually to exchange duties. This was not because I was dissatisfied with either; both had performed admirably. But I thought further continuance of established patterns would soon lead to their being frozen. The exchange was salutary. Both continued to do admirably; neither handled his new assignments just as his predecessor had; each got a fresh perspective on old and familiar problems.

This theory explains one reason why, as I look back over the years I served as a president, there was great variety in the parts of my own work that received emphasis at different times. When I was tired of doing the same things again and again, tasks which were necessary but had lost their challenge, I surrendered them to another officer and put my energies on other work, which, if not more useful, was at least more exciting—perhaps the same thing in the long run.

One of these duties was correspondence. A college president wades through seas of paper. The people who write to him seem to have a positive genius for prolixity, being able to enlarge a message worth a paragraph into pages. The amount and range of his correspondence is no less than astounding. An indication of the multiple character of the college presidency is the variety of things about which people write.

He hears about education in all its aspects—from preschool to adult education. That is normal enough, for the whole of education is one integral enterprise, despite its segmentation in management. He receives missives about politics, world affairs, economics, social conditions—at many levels of specificity and generality, superficiality and profundity. If someone has a plan for world peace, it will find its way to his desk, with a request he do something about it. If inflation threatens, or depression, or unemployment, why does he not take a position and "fix it"?

The morals, manners, customs, clothing of the younger generation are degenerate; will he not reverse the trend to decadence before it is too late, if it is not already? Too many victories in athletics bring sneering comments about recruitment, admission, and academic standards. Too few conquests in sports result in anguished cries that the prestige of the institution is imperiled—or destroyed, that the coach should be relieved of his post, that the athletic council is hostile to physical fitness, and so on and on and on. The alumnus complains that he never hears from the college save through an appeal for more money; "What have you done with the ten dollars I sent two years ago?" A trustee writes that the president is giving so much time to educational matters that promotion and fund raising are suffering; does he not know that standards are no substitute for solvency?

The list of comunications could be extended, without exaggeration, to a whole volume. What to do with it all? Save for two groups it must be answered. It is astounding what repercussions any apparent discourtesy can precipitate. The absolute cranks, and there are more of them than seems credible, constitute one group who can be ignored. Anonymous letters give no opportunity for reply; after some years of wading through them, I made a rule not to read them at all. Someone else could read them, file them for possible future reference, and refer the most violent, obscene, or threatening to the postal authorities.

The habit of dealing with the mail the first thing in the

morning is borrowed from business. It is one of the instances in which equating educational administration with business procedures is worse than irrelevant because the nature of the correspondence in the two enterprises is quite different. Business correspondence is predominantly about business—it is relevant to the principal preoccupation of such officers. College correspondence, on the other hand, is predominantly about everything in the world and nothing at all. Much of it is irrelevant to the president's principal preoccupation. For him to model his treatment of mail upon business practice is to fail to distinguish between two different sorts of situations.

I tried to read all the correspondence, not, I confess, with equal care and concentration. Nor did I read it all at once, or the first thing in the morning. The mail was opened by a secretary and classified by her or my assistant. Matters of urgent college importance were brought to my attention right away. Those constituted a very small proportion of the total. The rest must wait until my mind was clear of its own urgent concerns.

I have never been a good sleeper, and in the wakeful still of the night ideas sometimes take shape and crystallize. I tried every sort of device to capture them before they were erased by sleep. Sometimes I repeated the key phrases over and over to be sure to catch their exact form—the effort prolonged wakefulness and meant a jaded morning. A dictating machine had to be started, warmed, used with some light—and made me more wakeful. A friend gave me a pad which was lit by a battery bulb when the pencil was withdrawn from its place; that was best of all—it was at hand, it did not fill my eyes with light, it captured the idea before it fled—and in the form that relaxed contemplation had given it.

Sometimes in the morning these pre-dawn insights seemed

insipid to a degree; more often they triggered a train of thought that was absorbing and occasionally rewarding. On arrival at the office this was my first business—to round out and complete, if possible, what the night had begun. To let correspondence, mostly irrelevant and overwhelmingly trivial, break my train of thought proved to be foolish. Again and again the intrusion of some irate correspondence disrupted all coherence. It seems to me a president has a right to direct his own thoughts, rather than take his cue from some person at a distance who has spent a few cents to impose his will upon the harried administrator. Therefore, I learned to postpone till later everything that was not both primary and urgent. The first business was to clear my own mind.

The second thing about correspondence which hard experience taught me was that much could be answered better by someone else. If a communication deserved a response, it should have a good one. Preparation of such a reply might well require reference to the files for previous exchanges with the same person, or with others on the same or a related topic. Answering inquiries from memory can lead to a very red face. The letter may well represent a major interest of the correspondent, however marginal to the concern of the college president. The writer's memory on the matter at hand is likely to be more accurate. Only careful review of earlier letters can avoid mistakes, sometimes serious. The time and attention needed for that sort of work is seldom available to a president. For that reason the preparation of the response should be assigned to the person who can give it the concentrated thought it requires.

Who signs the letter depends upon circumstances. At times it is more polite—not to say more honest—to state frankly that the matter has been referred to another officer for reply. Some letters the president must sign; if he does not write them, he should make sure they carry his own authentic voice. That can be achieved by a phrase, a sentence, a paragraph. A skillful assistant can sometimes supply even those personal touches. In my last years at Brown, after discussion of a proposed letter with my assistant, he could draft it so much in my manner that I could not tell five or six weeks later which of us had actually chosen the words.

I learned these techniques when the Institute of Paper Chemistry was founded and I became its director. In a brand-new institution any letter may set—or tend to set—a policy. Therefore I read every letter in or out. As the Institute grew that became physically impossible, and I asked a brilliant young assistant—now President of the Institute—to digest the correspondence so that I might keep in intimate touch. During the eight years I directed the institution that process continued; as decentralization of tasks advanced I could still keep a firm grip upon policy. What necessity forced upon me there developed in a different—but equally rewarding—procedure at Brown.

After this process had matured I did not actually dictate more than ten percent of the responses to the mountains of mail. And that drafting was never done until the preoccupations of my over-night mind had been cleared in memo, in conference, in action, or in a speech. That word "dictate" in the first sentence is the key. For most college presidents, I discovered through the years, the daily correspondence dictated the course of their thought, action, and word. A horde of people, mostly at a great distance, decanted upon the president's desk a miscellaneous lot of uncoordinated—not to say incoherent—topics to which he sought to address his mind.

What nonsense that is as a program of administration. The first duty of a president is to direct his own mind and not make it subject to the dictation of people who have little or no responsibility for the management of the institution. Yet that is what the slave to the morning's mail submits to. It is the perfect program for disorganizing thought and making action incoherent. Excessive attention to the details of correspondence is one of the surest guarantees of boredom, which, as I have indicated many times in these pages, is the president's worst enemy.

The point made in an earlier chapter is worthy of being stressed again: the administrator is different from the scholar; he must often make up his mind and act before all the evidence is in. When, as research student, I wrote a book, nothing could hurry me until I found the answer. I might be (and was) under some pressure to publish, but was under no compulsion, so what I started about 1914 did not appear in book form until 1929. The administrator who operated with such meticulous deliberation could not function. He has to move —to act—on the best evidence available in the time permitted. But if he is to act wisely he must think, and thinking requires not only time but unhurried, uncluttered time.

This is another reason for decentralizing correspondence and interviews. People who had only a superficial acquaintance with me were always exclaiming that I acted rapidly; my intimate associates were always pressing for decisions that seemed to them postponed almost—if not quite—too long.

How could there be such a contrariety of view? It arose not from the substance, but the manner, of action. Many decisions are reached with difficulty and only after carefully weighing the evidence; with most important choices the pros and cons are closely balanced. Once the decision is made it is best to take a position as though there had never been any doubt. Otherwise proponents of a different course renew their efforts and the decision becomes undecided, administration wavers, falters, and ends in confusion. Firmness must not degenerate into stubbornness, but unless new evidence is adduced stability in a policy once adopted helps establish a pattern for the next problem. Stuttering is a painful speech defect; it is fatal to administration.

It is essential for a president to protect his time so that there is opportunity to read. In a sense the most insidious attack that can be made upon his competence is through the erosion of his reading habits. If he has been a scholar he must retain some interest in his specialty. Otherwise faculty members will begin to doubt he ever had any. They are inevitably somewhat suspicious of a man who turns from research and teaching to administration; they have a feeling that if those preoccupations had been really engrossing he would never have been seduced by administrative office. If he now neglects his field of study their suspicions will seem to be confirmed.

He must also save time to read educational literature—of many sorts. Unless he reads philosophical essays like those of Whitehead and Livingstone his own thinking will be dulled. He must read such works as Barzun's *Teacher in America* and Van Doren's *Liberal Education* to keep in touch with the thinking of operative men in the world of education. He must read about new methods of testing, measurement, vocational guidance, and a dozen other technical matters, else he will find himself way out of his depth in the curriculum committee. He must keep abreast of current affairs, for he is inescapably a public figure, and what he says on public matters will make him either controversial or dull. It is better to be disagreed with than neglected.

He should also show students that he can read outside his official preoccupations. I had this point driven home while I was at Lawrence. In a discussion with some seniors I inquired what they were reading; with one voice they said their normal work was so heavy that they had no time for recreational reading; they were "too busy." Almost as an act of desperation I challenged them: were they busier than I? They agreed they were not. So I asked how many would read as much as I did outside history, education, and current affairs. A considerable group volunteered. It was one of the most rewarding experiences I ever had with students. Several discovered that reading is a habit, and one that can be cultivated, that there is much time wasted which can be enjoyed by a program of reading. But the experiment was more important for me than for the students. It demonstrated that if I faltered in the pursuit of good reading any leadership I might have would be impaired.

There is a further reason why a president must prevent the pressures of administration from preempting his leisure for reading. He must talk. Heavens! how he must talk. He has three choices. He can say nothing, to the acute discomfort of his audience. Or he can repeat. This was the technique of one of the famous university presidents in the Midwest. He had six or eight stock speeches. They had been worn as smooth as stones in a brook—by the same process; they had been rolled over and over. They were held together in outline by mnemonic alliteration; he once explained it to me. They were delivered with the art of an actor who has recited the lines a thousand times. Yet despite his histrionic finish the fact remained that audiences got tired of even such deft repetition.

The third alternative is to fill the mind with fresh ideas by wide reading. It must be done in leisure, and in no acquisitive mood. If one reads to "find" speeches he will be plagiarizing—not crudely, perhaps—not in a manner to create a public scandal, but he will be speaking thoughts not actually his own. He should read in a relaxed and hospitable mood; the prayer book has a phrase, "read, learn, and inwardly digest." Digestion is the principal thing. What he reads must not be chunks swallowed whole, but transformed by intellectual digestion into his own thought and feeling. That process takes time, and is facilitated by a sense of calm and relaxation.

A mind so nourished is more likely to develop insights which, if not absolutely original, nonetheless have a freshness and vividness that would otherwise be lacking. Those qualities, which give life to a speech, cannot be guaranteed by any process. But if the root of the matter is there, this procedure supplies a proper environment for its development.

The president must not only find time to read, he must take time to write. A good speech is not dependent upon a "gift of gab." That may be essential equipment for a demagogue; but for an educator, trying to say something which will stir minds and move them to action, much more is required. Time spent in the preparation of a speech is usually a net subtraction from the pain both of delivery and reception.

I recall a new college president who was due to speak at a large dinner of educators. He had sketched out in his mind a parable. It had none of the innate simplicity such a figure requires if it is to be effective; indeed it had seven parts. The first one fell flat; the second was painful. By that time it was clear to the audience that it was in for a bad time; during the third part it had become equally manifest to the speaker. But he had announced seven points, and seven points he had to try to make. When he was getting ready, he thought he had a bright idea, and then, without further hard labor, attempted to extemporize. Preparation would have saved the audience acute embarrassment—and the president's reputation. The cynic who asserted that the best *ex tempore* speeches are those carefully memorized had a sound core to his remark.

Preparation takes time; when it is hurried it is inadequate.

Since most presidents have to make between fifty and a hundred speeches a year, the time required for the process of getting ready is considerable. For major addresses I liked to take about three months, putting down snatches occasionally, turning the whole matter over in peaceful moments until a pattern was formed. Then began the drafting, the revision, the redrafting until staff patience was wearing thin, and repetition threatened to stale my own taste for the subject.

This is a task, moreover, where delegation of responsibility is severely limited. I express my deep gratitude to reference librarians at Lawrence and Brown for the patient search for vaguely remembered quotations; and I owe an even deeper obligation to a research assistant who checked and rechecked, who was death on dangling participles and other involuntary deviations from the norm, whose critical eye and strong sense of order made clear points on which my exposition was foggy. By such means a president can get a lot of valuable help, and save himself precious time. But when all is said and done speech making is one place where he must do most of the work himself—and take all the responsibility. If he is answering unnecessary letters, and doing things others can do better than he, this essential part of his task will be short-changed—a loss to all concerned.

Money raising is another phase of his labors where delegation of responsibility is virtually impossible, and where there are severe limits even to the help he can get. An officer can run an alumni campaign; he can organize a "drive" on the occasions when that technique is called for; he can keep a prospect list, gather data about possible donors. Administrative detail and preparatory moves can be assigned to other people. But when it comes to asking for sizable sums, donors want the president to do it in person.

While I was living in New York helping President Shanklin, my opposite number in the Mt. Holyoke campaign related an incident the only unique aspect of which was its blunt candor. An alumna approached a famous and wealthy man in Chicago to ask for a subscription to the Mt. Holyoke fund; the response was frank to the point of being brutal: "I am accustomed to having college presidents do their begging in person." That particular tycoon put in plain words a view that is more common than not. Trustees can sometimes raise a great deal of money—if they will. But even in those instances the president has almost always to put in his oar.

Money raising I found to be by far the most arduous aspect of my job. Its demands were not so much physical, or even mental; the strain was on the nervous system and on one's character. When there is a large sum of money at stake—and for a good cause—it is hard not to cater to the whims of a prospective donor. To most of his notions there is no danger in yielding; they are harmless in that they do not affect the integrity of the educational enterprise. If he has a fancy—a whim of iron—about some architectural style it can be indulged unless it destroys an over-all plan, or swears with its surroundings. But when he wants to say what kind of economics is to be taught, or what philosophy, no compromise is available. It is necessary to withdraw as gracefully as possible—which may be fighting mad, underneath. There is no use in telling him the institution is not for sale; he would not understand the remark. From his point of view he is simply trying to have his money spent for purposes of which he approves. This may be a perfectly honest thought; he cannot see the collateral inferences.

Such cases are unusual. Far more common is the resistance of the self-styled "practical" individual who wants instruction to be "down to earth," and designed to "fit a man to earn an honest dollar." For some schools in a university and for some courses, this objective may be not only a permissible, but a sound program. It can be vicious, however, when it involves chiseling away at the liberal arts in a college.

In my experience crude instances are rare. But it is almost equally rare to find a generous donor who has a comprehensive vision of the educational enterprise as a whole, its deep significance for individual lives and the future of the nation. As I look back across the years, I have known a few such people, and they stand out like beacons. A gift from such a person is so heartening that it arouses new courage to try to kindle fires under damp twigs.

The president who gives too little time to money raising will never have a balanced budget, a salary increase for the faculty, or well-maintained buildings and grounds. The one who pours too much of his time and energy into fund accumulation will lose touch with the faculty, the curriculum, the students—and even worse, with ideas. No man can write a prescription to tell another how much is too much, how little is not enough. The balance is the fruit of experience—hard experience.

The relationship of the president to the budget is a strange mixture of delegation of authority and personal control. It would be beyond human power for him to "make" the budget all by himself. It is far too complicated a task; there simply are not enough hours in the day or enough days available to permit such a course of action. Decentralization is the first necessity; only by such methods can the vast mass of requisite data be gathered and put in reviewable order. Delegation is the second essential; the business office must collate, organize, calculate, and predict. Advice is the third step; without help no president can know enough to make the enormous range of decisions required to arrive at wise conclusions. This assistance must come from departmental chairmen, from deans who are responsible for the first review of sections appropriate to their realms of action, from officers dealing with maintenance and operation of the plant.

How orderly and rational that sounds! Usually the process is less so than the description. In 1958 a parliamentary committee, inquiring into Treasury control of expenditures by the British government, and calling for reform, remarked: "Examination of the estimates may tend to be concentrated on those that have increased, and the possibilities of economies in those that are static, or of greater economies in those which have decreased, may be neglected." Although new policies which will cost money are examined toughly, there is no regular method to prevent a policy from "living on its legend and going on because it was approved four or five years ago." Those words could have been written by any college president who has wrestled with a long succession of budgets brought to him in draft form by the business office.

What is the function of the president in this annual scramble for pennies? First of all he must have in mind a clear order of priorities. If he and others connected with the institution are alert to educational opportunity, the college or university, whatever its "wealth," will never have enough money to do all that could well be done. Any time a president boasts that "our resources are adequate for our program" you can be certain that the program is impoverished. With all that needs to be accomplished in regard to respectable faculty salaries, improved ratio of faculty to students, better library assets more readily available, laboratories modernly equipped, residences and dining halls to supplement rather than obstruct education, and buildings and grounds adequate to their purpose, money will always be short.

If a president had to deny only foolish and wasteful requests for appropriations the task, assuming he had reasonable experience and wisdom, would be relatively easy. Stress is on the word "relatively." In actual practice he must refuse appropriations for proposals not only legitimate but wise and forward looking.

It is at this point that his priorities must begin to function. As the draft budget comes to him he must spot the program which is "living on its legend," and balance its continuance against new proposals which may offer greater promise of educational advance. If he does not do this, the educational program begins rapidly to ossify, and all the work of a curriculum committee, all the insights of some alert professor cannot stop the process. If every new idea must wait upon increased resources so that it may be piled atop all the old procedures, the situation soon becomes hopeless.

However, novelty is no guarantee of wisdom, nor age of sterility among ideas. The most difficult of all decisions requiring keen discernment and flexibility and courage are the choices of priorities. They are scarcely ever publicized —or even known outside a very small group. But they are vastly more important than most of those which hit the headlines.

The second duty of the president as he approaches the draft budget is to make sure that it does not rob Peter—the capital assets—to pay Paul—the current deficit. This is an insidious temptation. With all the pressure to balance the budget from the businessmen on the board of trustees it is easy to omit inevitable current expenses that do not have to be met "this year," or to take income from investments this year at the expense of some future year on the principle of "after me the deluge."

For example, dormitory furniture has only a moderately long life. There is inevitable depreciation each year—a proper charge against the current budget. For reasons growing out of tax exemption, absence of "profits," and other factors, colleges and universities do not usually have depreciation accounts. Nevertheless, they should have an equivalent

—current fund reserves. Both at Lawrence and at Brown I found dormitory furniture and kitchen equipment in bad shape, and no reserves available to pay for replacement. The budget of any single year could not meet the costs.

In one case recourse was had to borrowing and amortizing the expense over a period of years. The net effect was to increase the expenditure by the amount of the interest charge and to be forever behind. The better way, established at the first possible moment, was an annual appropriation to a replacement reserve. That reduced the cost because the reserve could be invested and earn money until needed for use. But unless I was alert the item would disappear on the ground that "we are not planning to buy any furniture next year, and we need the money to help balance the budget."

Another sample will illustrate the president's function. Every institution must purchase property from time to time. Failure to buy when it is on the market means paying a high price when it is needed and the owner is reluctant to sell. I recall with acute pain paying twenty thousand dollars for a narrow but essential strip when I had been unable to persuade the treasurer to buy the whole estate—twenty times as much land—for twelve thousand only a couple of years before.

However, when property can be bought, money is seldom available. Plant funds rarely have free balances! Thus there is a temptation to make purchases as "investment." Since the property is ultimately for plant use, it is labeled "temporary investment" but no provision is made for its amortization. The most extraordinary example of this occurred when such a purchase was held for fifteen years and an annual "revenue" of twenty percent was collected; when plant needed the property, it had to be "bought"—with new funds —from endowment. Hard experience of that kind taught me to make certain that properties purchased by one fund for use by another should have some systematic method of transfer—with a minimum of pain. No one but the president can scrutinize the accounts for such instances.

The president has a third function in connection with the budget. College endowments and assets consist of a vast number of separate funds—there are endowed professorships (almost always inadequate), all kinds of scholarships, loan funds, library funds. The entries run into the hundreds, and in larger institutions into thousands; each carries with it, by will or by other instrument, limitations upon its investment, its use, the handling of balances—an almost infinite number of details.

Such restrictions often make it difficult to spend the income in strict accord with the terms. When a fund is old, when there is no one to challenge the use to which it is put, when no "adverse interest" is apparent, it is easy to rationalize breaches of the trust—"it is in a good cause" ! It is the president's business to remember that they are trusts, and that they must never be abused. There is always an appeal to the courts if a fund becomes unusable, but the maintenance of good faith with donors is essential.

On the other side, while sometimes difficult, it is seldom impossible to expend the income while observing the terms of the trust. A study of treasurers' reports occasionally shows somewhat astonishing sums lying idle, so far as performing their appropriate function is concerned, for lack of resourcefulness and imagination in their utilization. When a president discovers funds piling up unused income it is his business to incorporate that income into the budget and put it to work, if at all possible.

The budget is one of the most important instruments of management. Handling it in a casual or routine manner means surrendering one of the few sources of influence and power available to a president. He cannot "make" the budget; he cannot even review every item; but he can—and must—set policies, determine priorities, scrutinize it critically to insure fullest and wisest use of available income.

The powers of a president as chief administrator are considerable. Most people think of them as overwhelming. Some, who have had their requests trimmed or refused, are inclined to say with Edmund Burke, "Power gradually extirpates from the mind every humane and gentle virtue." I have heard other presidents—and myself—described in those terms, or similar ones, from time to time. There must occasionally be some truth in those allegations, as there is in the common aspersions upon presidential veracity. But while the power is real it is much less than is usually supposed. No matter how alert a president may be, he is hedged about by a bureaucracy which narrows the range of his free judgment. He is restrained, also, by the political nature of his office; he can say "No" only so often before resistance is stimulated to the point of becoming effective. He can set his judgment over and above advice for only a limited time and in limited areas before complaints to trustees make his position so weak as to approximate impotence.

The president must use power economically, and persuasion to the fullest extent. The quality which he can never use sparingly is energy. A president needs wisdom, experience, warmth, sympathy, insight; indeed one can pile on descriptive words indefinitely. He will not have all those desirable qualities. But to be successful he must have energy. The office is an exhausting one; I observed that in my first contacts with it as an undergraduate. I learned it all over again when I was President Shanklin's assistant. Then the lesson was heaped up, pressed down, and running over after I took office.

When a man's energy begins to flag and a vacation does not restore it, the time has come to retire. I have seen many presidents who felt their accumulated wisdom, experience, and judgment were so great that they could continue to hold office and delegate providing the energy to others, so to speak. That conclusion may have been justified in some instances. I never observed one; in every case that came under my notice the result was not only to impair—or destroy—the man's reputation; that could be borne. The consequence was damage to the institution. Its machinery requires great energy to make it move with speed and precision. The president cannot, of course, supply all the energy. But he sets the pace; when his pace slackens he should turn the job over to another.

V

The Students

THE relationship of a college president to the students is difficult to describe. Its complexity is one reason. But far more important in obscuring this vital segment of a president's duties is the aura of myth that surrounds the whole subject. The college president, in the dominant tradition, is close to the students—a presence. He is at once the illuminating teacher, the great inspiration, the awful disciplinarian, and the kindly, warm-hearted friend who loans students money, forgives academic deficiencies because of profound faith in youth. He is a man of stature, dressed to the full height of his dignity and authority, always at the student's side, yet in the midst of every student brawl to break it up.

Traditions do not come from nowhere; consequently there must have been prototypes of this mythical character. Perhaps "Benny" Andrews of Brown was such a one. He seems to have dominated the college, to have awakened fierce loyalties among many students and equal antipathies among some trustees. He was omnipresent in classroom, in chapel, in sports, in riots.

Two other men may be thought to approach the image. Kenneth Charles Morton (Casey) Sills headed Bowdoin for over thirty years and earlier had been professor and dean. He embodied, in many respects, the history and tradition of his college; for a long time he was the only real officer—the dean had a desk in his office. The college was small enough so that he could know most of the students as he taught them and lived among them. Ernest Martin Hopkins left a personal impress at Dartmouth—so deep as to be almost tangible.

Possibly other illustrations which in some respects approximate the mythical image could be adduced. I was never personally acquainted with a president who met all the specifications. It seems clear to me that the persistent tradition is not constructed about individual men; it is a montage, pictures of many men superimposed, the salient characteristics of the strongest among them dominating the result.

The actual relationship of a president to students will vary with his age, with the size and character of the institution, as well as with his personality.

If a man is "young" when he begins his presidency, as I was, there is a possibility of achieving some brief intimacy. "Young" belongs in quotation marks because to students of eighteen to twenty years thirty-six is an advanced age. But when thirty-six succeeds sixty-six, the change is marked enough so that, for a moment, students regard the new president as "young." For a moment—those are the words to stress. The next freshman class never knew the sixty-six-year-old. What is more startling, they never heard of him. To them he is less familiar than George Washington or Napoleon Bonaparte. The near past is as dead as the far past to freshmen. To them the new president is as though he had always been there, and certainly not young—by any standard which is meaningful to them.

That first year the new president may appear to be almost "one of the boys." He can go to the locker room before a football game and give a pep talk to the squad. He can dance with students without evoking jeering comment behind his back. There can be a kind of camaraderie. But if he is perceptive he will discover how transient is this era in his relationships. He will find true what Charles Flandrau wrote at the end of the last century about an instructor named Thorn, whose effort to be a bridge between students and faculty ended in bitter disillusionment. He knew the students. "But they didn't know him. Nor did it ever occur to them that they wanted to or could. They were not seeking the maturer companionship Thorn had to give. . . . They took life as they found it near at hand, and Thorn was far, very far away." He learned, at last and with pain, "to understand something of the fine line that separates instructor from instructed, *on whose other side neither may trespass*."

The fundamental basis of the president's contacts with undergraduates must be professional; his objective must be their respect; he must accept the age gap as a solid fact and not pretend to a youth the students know full well he has lost. Whatever his affection for them, he must not, save in rare cases, expect affection in return. And he will be wise not to speak of his affection—or show it too plainly. If he does, he will be set down as a sentimental old fool, and maybe correctly. The students do not want his affection. His feelings toward them should be dominated by respect—as theirs toward him—respect for their desire for privacy, respect for their character, respect for their minds. This respect must be realistic; it is not realistic to see students through a purple haze, or as plaster saints. That leads to heartbreak.

This professional attitude does not preclude warm friendships with some students. Such relationships may grow under any number of normal circumstances through which a few undergraduates are brought into close personal touch—such as teaching, employment as "baby sitters" or part-time chauffeurs, or as a result of acquaintance with parents—in an almost infinite variety of ways. They will be—considering the whole number of students—exceptional, and never familiar.

A professional contact does not always have to be solemn. I knew, at Lawrence, that when I was out of earshot (and occasionally when they did not know I could hear) the students customarily referred to me as "Hank." So, when I was trying to make commencement more orderly and impressive, I told the seniors that no one who forgot to shift the tassel of his mortar board at precisely the proper moment could ever address me directly in that fashion. It produced a reaction almost military in its precision; the tassel went over and there came the murmured "good-bye, Hank"—a daring act!

Lawrence was small enough so that I could know nearly every student and something personal about each. It gave warmth and relaxation of tension when with the diploma went some word of greeting and farewell. But such episodic incidents were, so to speak, frosting on the cake. The fundamental contact was professional, even when some personal element was added.

The size of the institution affects profoundly the relationship of students to the president. At Brown and Pembroke there were too many students to make knowing them all—or even a major share—a practical possibility. Moreover, there was a screen of deans between undergraduates and me—perhaps an even denser barrier between graduate students and me. As a matter of sound administration the president must be exceedingly careful not to trespass upon the functions of the deans. Any student has a right to appeal to the president from the decision and action of any dean; that is fundamental to administrative order. But the exercise of this right must come only as a true appeal, not as a trip up the back stairs, leaving the dean out of the contact. The "campus lawyers," undergraduates of a litigious disposition, were forever trying to by-pass the dean as "prejudiced," "unsympathetic"—add adjectives to taste—in order to involve the president directly in their concerns.

Parents occasionally attempted like sharp practice. One of the most absurd occurred at a commencement reception. About two thousand people came down the line that day—a sufficiently exhausting experience without all the other things a president has to do during that long week end. But one couple stopped the whole proceeding to demand an interview; their son was being tragically abused. As tactfully as possible I pointed to the dean standing at another spot on the lawn, and said he was the first court of appeal. Without tact they refused to see the dean; no one but the president could right so monstrous a wrong; in any event the dean did not look sympathetic! The line was showing marked evidences of impatience; if I was not it was a histrionic triumph. I caught the eye of my assistant—a very present help in time of trouble—and asked him to take over. He led the protesting pair away, steered them to the dean, and made an appointment for them to return to see me in the evening. What was the tragic circumstance? Their son was graduating *magna cum laude;* they wanted a *summa* and felt I could confer it, all requirements to the contrary notwithstanding.

Usually those who sought to by-pass the deans, whether undergraduates or parents, were up to just that sort of shenanigans. Even true appeals from the acts of the deans were customarily over minor rather than major issues. Nevertheless it was necessary to hear the complaints, sift the evidence, and judge the issue fairly. In ninety-nine cases out of a hundred the decision upheld the dean. Sometimes, when the weight of the evidence was so nearly equal as to make no conclusion obvious, the dean's decision was confirmed in order not to erode his authority and encourage frivolous appeals. In the rare instances where his decision was modified or reversed, the action was taken in conference with him, with his assent—and when possible announced by him.

One of the most difficult of all techniques was the maintenance of an open door for students without impairing the authority of their normal academic or disciplinary superiors. A way to achieve that end was to encourage students to come in to talk of their educational or vocational plans. This involved no trespass upon any officer's duties—or feelings. At the same time it gave an opportunity in the casual conversation that preceded and followed the specific topic of the student's concern to sample campus opinion and the state of student morale.

There was a time at Lawrence when I was harassed by a student conviction that my office managed a spy system. The rumor—which grew to "certainty"—arose naturally enough. It seemed to some students that I could not know so much about them as individuals, or of student affairs generally, without the help of informers. The dilemma was painful. It is of the first importance for an administrator to know what is going on in the college; it is fatal to effectiveness to have the break in morale that spying—or belief that there is spying —precipitates. A demonstration of my methods was the only possible cure.

The knowledge that mystified them had come from the students themselves. They had little realization of the way in which they babbled when they talked. Much of what they said was trivial and superficial, but amid the torrent of unconsidered words were pieces of information—what I have called elsewhere the undertones and overtones of their conversation. It was no trick at all, after hearing a few, to divine what was afoot in student life. One or two practical illustrations of the inferences to be drawn in such circumstances cleared up the "spying" charge. Even such a candid demonstration of method did not close the source of information, for students love to talk and discretion is not the principal characteristic of young people—even in their latest teens and early twenties.

Another step was necessary to assure cordial working relations. It was made perfectly clear to responsible student leaders that the information assembled was not used to "catch" people in order to discipline them. On the contrary, the objective was to forestall trouble and escape the need for punishment. My point of view had grown out of my experience with the "rogues and rascals" of whom I saw so much while teaching at Wesleyan. Every difficulty anticipated and avoided was better than ten instances of punishment meted out—however justly—after a foreseeable situation had been allowed to mature into real trouble that could not be overlooked.

A device to this end was the appointment of young assistants, lately enough out of college not be handicapped by the age gap. Their instructions were to take the pressure off the dean and me by identifying prospective areas of friction and putting on the essential drop of oil—a clear hint—before the heat was sufficiently intense to light the tinder that always lies about a campus. One instance of discipline made unnecessary by foresight is better than a dozen cases of "punishment" so far as student morale is concerned.

It is sometimes assumed that students have no interest in the curriculum or other academic requirements. From one point of view, that of details, this is true. But in a larger and more significant sense it is essential that the regulations, and their administration, should be such as to evoke respect.

In my class in college one of the seniors who lived in the same house with me took an entrance examination in mathematics on commencement morning. He had been admitted "on condition"; subsequently he had passed his college mathematics and met all the requirements for graduation; but he had never formally removed the "condition." The diplomas were all signed, the program printed—but there was a blank space on his card; academic bureaucracy could not rest until there was a check mark in that empty square. Everyone knew that the "examination" was a farce, and would probably never be graded. It was a ceremonial gesture to a concept of education that made no sense at all. The fact that the episode has lived in my memory for forty-seven years—and stayed with the "victim" as long as he lived—reveals its utter stupidity. It may be one of the roots of my suspicion of registrars.

This may seem to be an extreme example. Perhaps it is in that precise form; but the substance of such folly I have had occasion to observe many times. Indeed it requires continuous alertness to extirpate such nonsense. Unless the effort is made students lose respect for the institution. They do not resent high standards; in fact, however much they grouse, they glory in them. Raising standards is one of the quickest and best ways to improve morale and build a sense of pride and a feeling of loyalty. But niggling bureaucratism is not enforcement of standards; it is just absurdity.

Student pride is essential. One of the great strengths of the Ivy group is not the reality of their high standards (which are not greatly superior to those of many good institutions) but the realization on the part of the undergraduate that he is a "citizen of no mean city." In the Middle West in the late twenties absence of such an awareness was a great educational handicap to the colleges; the state universities were so dominant that all other institutions were denigrated automatically to second grade.

It jolted me severely; no one at Wesleyan had any sense of academic inferiority; at Williams, where I spent several summers at the Institute of Politics, there was no evidence of any such feeling. But in Wisconsin it was so real as to be palpable. It affected not only students but faculties. I was amazed when, in curriculum committee, proposals were not discussed on their merits but debate turned on acceptability for transfer to the university. There was a marked effort to "keep in step," lest some course would not be given "credit" when a transfer was made.

It must be said that the state university pursued policies of academic imperialism; it showed no eagerness to have truly independent colleges, but seemed to use its great prestige to make them satellites. For example, a Lawrence student sought to transfer to the university. He had taken a course in spoken English in his freshman year. The university declined to accord credit for it on the ground that it was taken in a different year from that in which a like course was offered in Madison. The immediate inference by the boy and his parents was that Lawrence was doing something educationally wrong. The family was influential—and vocal; they stirred up a row of serious proportions. Whereupon I hied me to Madison to protest to the dean that the university was needlessly injuring a sister institution.

His reply was completely cynical. He conceded that the subject was a proper freshman study; there was nothing wrong, he admitted, with the Lawrence course. But it was an expensive course; it required that time be spent with individual students. If the university granted credit for such instruction taken elsewhere, there would be pressure for the teaching of oral English in the freshman year in Madison. Inasmuch as about half the entering class would be dropped from the university at the end of the first year, it was not wise to give such an expensive course. If that administrative decision injured another institution, it was no concern of his.

He explained that this action was not "discriminatory." Wisconsin had requested the University of Chicago to accept, as juniors, any students who had finished the work in

Dr. Meiklejohn's two-year "experimental college." Chicago agreed. But when a Chicago student offered the famous course in "The Nature of the World and of Man" for credit at Wisconsin the request was declined.

I was furious. The fact that the university's action was not "discriminatory" did not interest me in the slightest; the fact that it was undiscriminating did. I returned to Appleton determined to break the lock step, to set up a curriculum of our own that would not dovetail with that of the university —to "go it alone" and let the consequences be what they would. Lawrence made it clear that, while it would not bar from admission students who intended to transfer later, it would not be hospitable to their applications and would do nothing whatever to facilitate those plans. That move, together with a number of other evidences of independence, such as dropping "business administration," sharply reduced the size of the freshman class, but it markedly increased the size of the upper classes. It greatly improved the balance of the student body; it bettered instruction in the last two years. And it notably raised the academic morale of students.

There is reputed to be an old Scotch prayer: "God gie us a gude conceit of oursells." I recommend it as a daily exercise. The colleges that have gone their own way in the Middle West are those whose reputations among the public, and even more among their students, have most improved. Self-respect is essential to winning the respect of others.

Another dramatic step contributed to the surge in student morale at Lawrence. The college announced that no one who failed of acceptance elsewhere or who was advised to leave an institution would be admitted. This was a far more drastic step than appears at first glance. Anyone familiar with academic matters is keenly aware that admission "standards" are far from precise. The fact that a student is declined admission to one college and accepted at another does not necessarily mean that the standards of the former are higher; more often it reflects differences in judgments of two admission officers, who might, on some other day, reach just the opposite conclusion. Nevertheless the public, unaware of any such subjectivity of opinion, will assume that the college which accepts this student "will take anyone." Institutions with firmly established prestige can shrug off such inferences; those seeking to win a secure status cannot.

Refusal to admit everyone declined elsewhere was not "fair" to some individuals; but the boost in morale of those admitted was sufficiently great to make it a desirable step—temporarily. It must be remembered that education cannot be "given" to a student; therefore his emotional approach is of first importance. If he has confidence in his college, even more if he has pride, his receptivity is heightened. Everything which strengthens his assurance in the validity of the program he is following is worth doing. The more he grouses about it being "tough to get in and tough to stay in," the more his response is sharpened.

Academic discipline and control of behavior should never be confused. Yet at one point they meet—the dismissal of a student from college. The story, perhaps apochryphal, is told of a conversation between Woodrow Wilson when president of Princeton and an overanxious mother. She was asking that special care be given her son's education. "Madame," said Wilson, "we guarantee satisfaction or return the boy." It was a profound observation. Education, I repeat, is a voluntary matter. No "requirement" can be forced; the undergraduate may simply sit idle, or he may carouse; he may lack ability for the kind of independent work a college should demand. Under those circumstances he belongs at home.

If a college cannot serve a student intellectually it cannot serve him at all. There are better rest homes and recreation centers elsewhere; an institution of higher education has no obligation to substitute for either. Nor is it the duty of a college to reform a student's morals or even his manners. Of course, in the words of the Brown Charter, there is concern that "above all, a constant regard be paid to, and effectual care taken of, the morals of the College."

Certainly nothing should be done—or tolerated—that will debauch the morals of the student. But behavior, like learning, is a voluntary act. All the rules in the world will not improve a rotten egg. While, therefore, the environment must stimulate proper behavior, as it forwards intellectual effort, the college is not an institution for reform. It should strengthen character, but it cannot supply fundamental decency.

Moreover, in a society as intimately gregarious as undergraduate life tends to be, too much patience with a student who cannot or will not make the grade, or who will not behave himself, reduces the service which can be rendered those able and willing to discipline themselves. The salutary effect of the removal of the idle and the ill-behaved upon the balance of the student body is conspicuous. When an effort is being made to set a proper tone for the college, tolerance of one discordant note can be serious. Woodrow Wilson's promise to "return the boy" was a sound program. The obligation, as the Brown Charter so admirably emphasizes, is to the whole group—"the morals of the College."

An enormous lot of nonsense is uttered about dismissal from college. How many times have I heard the plea: "It will kill my mother." My customary response was to inquire why the student had never before shown, by his conduct, concern for her health. In thirty years of oiling the springs so the doors of the institution would swing outward freely

I never heard of an instance where any drastic change in parental well-being followed the dismissal of a son or daughter.

Almost as often I was told: "This will ruin my life; no one will give me a second chance." That plea is sheerest nonsense. There are dozens of institutions so avid for students, even in this crowded era, that there is always a second—and a third, sometimes a fourth—chance available. During the depression, and in many other periods, those who were dropped were not only admitted elsewhere, they were welcomed.

Despite anything one can do, it is hard to persuade undergraduates that the college does not "make money" from them. If the rumor gets started that there is hesitancy to drop a student lest revenue be lost the consequences are demoralizing. I observed this effect in the case of a college during the depression. Like many another it had built dormitories with borrowed money, borrowing so large a share of the cost that a second mortgage was "sold" to its own endowment. An empty room meant not only loss of direct revenue to service the first mortgage bonds, it had the added result of reducing endowment income—already too meager. The word went round the student body that if you could pay your room rent and board you could stay in college. The effect upon both morals and morale was deplorable.

That instance was conspicuous but not unique. After the First World War there was a surge of students. In the "Roaring Twenties" many colleges built too costly structures with too little equity. In one case a chapel and a stadium were constructed and "rented" pending annuity expiry or a bequest. When the Great Depression came there were many institutions which not only cut faculty salaries, they paid other bills first—to remain "solvent"—and gave the faculty whatever was left. To have expected them to "return the boy" would have been unreasonable. The Second World War stripped colleges of many of their students. Those that had not been conservative in financing new construction again found themselves badly squeezed, and in no position to exercise disciplinary control which reduced income.

In all the outcry that ensued upon the first Sputnik this history was never mentioned. Yet I am convinced that the patent and even more the subtle deterioration of standards during those two critical periods—depression and war—have left a legacy of lowered educational requirements in a great many institutions. Now, again, we are entered upon an era of rapid building and some pretty fancy financing. It seems safe enough because of the "flood" of students about to descend upon colleges and universities. But even more important than expansion is the recovery of the power and the courage to "return the boy" who is not getting a real education because of lack of talent or want of will to self-discipline. The need of the world is for more well educated men and women, not just more holders of degrees.

Most of the lesser forms of discipline are futile or worse. To grant an extended absence—by "suspension"—to a boy who is chronically "away" makes no sense at all. When a student is habitually absent and is then "suspended," it makes his recovery of academic health more doubtful; he is likely to become one of the scholastic "cripples" who clog our colleges. When such discipline is for moral delinquency the result, from his point of view, is a reward in the form of an extra vacation, and it increases the likelihood that he will be an academic as well as a moral casualty. Of all the sterile discussions I have heard in my years of office those whose "object all sublime" was to "make the punishment fit the crime" were the dreariest. The students who should be accorded respect are those who want an education, not those who only pay money rather than make an effort of mind and will.

The president is responsible for the tone of the discipline both scholastic and behavioral. If he has a philosophy behind his action and is humane but firm, he will soon see patterns established which conform to his ideas—if not quite to his ideals. Undoubtedly there must be a faculty committee, but its function should be that of watch-dog, not administration. Once administrative work is given to a committee it is assigned to the worst imaginable mechanism. Discipline of whatever kind succeeds best when it is prompt, consistent, and firm. To expect those qualities from a committee with changing personnel is hopeless. The dean should be the active figure. He will need advice from the faculty group, he will need support from the president.

Policy regarding scholarships and loans must also find its source in the president. This is no simple matter. The number of students involved and the sums of money committed and expended are both very large—and growing larger year by year. It is no longer possible for the president—or anyone else—to know enough about every applicant to deal fairly, generously—but economically—with each one. If grants are to be made wisely, the procedures are extremely complex. Those who have long been concerned with this phase of college administration are familiar with the loud protestations of poverty on the part of the well-to-do and the silence of the teachers and preachers too modest to make demands. The argument that without scholarship aid the family cannot have a second car may seem strange to the uninitiated, but it is common enough. Indeed it is by no means unheard of to find a request for scholarship aid so that the recipient may have a car at college.

Today most colleges require a rather full disclosure of the real financial situation of every applicant. Frequently that is checked by some credit organization such as serves stores and other enterprises that grant credit. These procedures are essential for all too many people think of colleges as "rich" (have they not millions in assets?) and therefore able to grant any sum desired.

I well remember a conversation with a successful businessman. He wanted to pay for his daughter's room, board, and tuition in monthly installments. The business manager said that would be quite satisfactory; there would be an interest charge on the due and unpaid balances. The man was outraged, stormed out of the business office, and insisted on seeing me—at once, with emphasis. I asked if he did any installment selling in his business; of course he did. Did he make a charge heavier than when cash was paid at the time of purchase? Of course, why not? When I inquired what the difference was in the two situations his answer was classic: one was business, the other education. I remained firm; then he appealed to me on what was supposed to be a soft spot; if he paid all at once, he would have to borrow at the bank—and pay interest. He could not see why deferred payments amounted to borrowing from the college.

That man was more nearly typical than unique. He stands out in my memory because he was a prosperous businessman, yet had a financial double standard—one for business, a wholly different set of principles for education. How common that attitude has been is evidenced by two simple sets of figures. While the American people have gone into installment debt for tangibles, such as cars, stoves, washing machines, television sets, and so on, to the tune of over thirty billion dollars, borrowing to pay educational costs—from all sources—probably does not approach half a billion. Every college officer is aware of the demand for grants and the reluctance to use loans "because I do not want to go into debt." A few questions soon reveal that the families already have installment debts for many other things. It is a distressing indication of their sense of relative values.

So strong has this tendency been that a decade ago there were literally millions of dollars in loan funds held by universities and colleges with a very weak market for them, though the call for scholarships remained insistent. All sorts of devices have been resorted to in order to put these funds to work. The commonest is to link the grant of a scholarship to willingness to accept a loan, and to set up some reasonable proportion between the two forms of student financing. As I was preparing to write this book I asked the president of one of the great and "well-endowed" institutions what the situation was now, for I had seen a treasurer's report some years ago that showed amazingly large idle loan funds. His answer was that pressure exerted by the linking of grant and loan had now put all those funds to work.

Where there is so much resistance to borrowing, there is certain to be great pressure for grants. Without the most thoroughgoing investigation of the real needs of applicants the money would go in large part to those recipients who least need it.

Sound administration gives great weight to talent and industry in making grants of any kind. Since tuition does not cover costs—in many state institutions it amounts to only a very tiny fraction of the cost—there is a general subsidy for every student enrolled; that means "financial help" to those of marginal ability and those willing to do only a minimum of work. Surely special subsidies should be reserved for the better students—better in terms of scholastic excellence and strength of character.

It is the business of the president to make certain that mechanical decisions do not replace perceptive judgment. A specific case—a real one—illustrates the point. A girl of fine abilities and a talent for leadership came to college—with almost no money at all. She had a scholarship, and a loan, and took as much part-time work as she could get. She did very well scholastically and began to play an important part in student self-government. Then she fell ill, got behind in her earnings, and upon her recovery tried to recoup her finances with more work. Her grades fell off somewhat, and under the inspiration of the registrar's statistics her scholarship was reduced in amount "because her academic standing did not warrant the larger figure." The inevitable result would have been to force her to give up her leadership in student life—a loss to the college—when she took on more work and lost more scholarship aid. The "rules" had become the enemy of sound practice. The decision was set aside, her scholarship grant increased. Her grades improved enough to "justify" the larger amount and her influence upon the student body was strengthened.

Rules can work damage in another direction. A case of "prejudice" was appealed to me. A candidate had been "denied admission" though his intelligence quotient was outstanding. It was asserted that the social standing of his parents—a minus quantity—had influenced the decision. The facts were different. He had not been denied admission; on the contrary he had been notified of acceptance. He had been refused scholarship aid. A first-hand investigation convinced me that the decision was correct; deficiencies in character did not warrant a further investment of endowed funds in a subsidy for him. Nevertheless, as a sop to misguided public opinion, I overruled the decision and made a substantial scholarship grant—but with stipulations regarding conduct to which he assented willingly. He agreed that unless he behaved the scholarship should not be renewed. He broke every promise he made; he continued to misbehave without any change; yet because his grades were high his scholarship aid was not terminated, but actually increased, and he was carried virtually tuition free for four years. No one brought the matter to my attention because there was no "adverse interest"—except education. The registrar's slide rule triumphed over not only good judgment but any judgment at all.

In another place I have discussed student residences and dining halls. There is, however, one further point that should receive special stress. It is the essentiality of stimulating the student to have a private life of the mind. If I had been able to find money enough, every dormitory I had anything to do with would have been made up of single rooms—no doubles, much less suites for three or four. Single rooms constitute no danger that undergraduates will not "learn how to live with other people." Their lives are much too gregarious; even if they have one room where privacy is possible they will still have enough group experience to avoid becoming antisocial. There are dormitory organizations for social life, intramural sports, self-government, and even discussions with faculty members and others. For many or most there is fraternity life as well.

But quite apart from these social aspects of gregariousness, and in my mind rather more serious, is the fact that the students' intellectual life has almost no privacy, not to say solitude. They meet in classes; they have common texts; they are examined together. Intellectually there is altogether too much togetherness. When it is time to study, or to write, in most instances it is by the sufferance of a roommate. He may want to listen to the radio, to play records, to play cards, to talk—to do any of numberless things which interfere with study. This is bad enough in its effect upon serious work; it is infinitely more disrupting to recreational reading. In matters of room arrangement, pictures, decoration of any kind individual taste must be subordinated to the wishes of another.

We have become so utterly gregarious that the desire of a great actress from Sweden, some years ago, "to be alone" became a by-word. It showed that she was peculiar—to many any such desire bordered on the abnormal. There is no danger that colleges will ever cultivate individual isolation; the manifest danger, plain to all with eyes to see, is that the individual will come to be lonely by himself, will need the stimulation of others to learn, or even to enjoy himself. A great educational reform desperately needed is the cultivation of a private life of the mind. To that purpose a galaxy of changes are essential: more stress on writing, more oral expression of ideas, more individual work under tutorial supervision, more recreational reading, more individual sports, and a place to live that assures, or at least permits, some measure of privacy.

It is one of the tragedies of our time that almost all the pressure on college administration is in the other direction. Alarm, amounting too often to panic, about the approaching flood of students is promoting more and more mass procedures, larger classes, less personal contact, additional mechanical "aids," more of everything that tends to overwhelm, rather than stimulate, a private life of the mind.

There is no other focal point for resistance to these trends save the president. If he takes a stand on behalf of the individual he will discover that many people deplore the lack of personal initiative, the tendency of the mass mind to dominate politics, the entertainment world, marketing—and a whole list of things every reader can supply from his own experience. But they are the same people who want education to be standardized, mass produced—and above all economical.

The plain, unadorned, cold fact is that "information," data, mental stuffing of many kinds can be transmitted in that manner. The equally plain—though unacknowledged—reality is that the higher mental processes needed in science, the humanities, the social studies, and the arts cannot be so produced. Progress in developing those higher mental processes is distinctively individual. At the risk of alienating some assent to my argument I will say bluntly it requires rugged individualism. We cannot mass produce poets, or Nobel Prize winners, or political thinkers; all those are individuals who think for themselves—and uniquely. They can never attain their personal goals or perform their reasonable service to society unless they are given the opportunity for, and a stimulus to, a private life of the mind.

I lived and worked among students for just short of fifty years. Every imaginable complaint I have heard. I listened —without any response save defiance—to the older generation denounce the ubiquitous whipcords and the peg-top trousers that were respectively the every day uniform and the dress up uniform of my undergraduate years. Later I heard—unmoved—the denunciation by my own generation of youths' dirty saddle shoes, then of blue jeans, and girls' shorts. Though I was in the last class at Wesleyan which followed the strict old classical curriculum, I was told it had already gone soft—and my generation was softer. Later I have heard the "younger generation" scolded and nagged and worried over.

The net effect upon me of that long experience is one of admiration for students. They follow the fads, different fads from those of their elders—but the fads are transitory, and superficial. Their language is no longer the same—they do not say such things as "23 skidoo." Their music doesn't go round and round, but up and down. They are not harmoniously concerned with the scarcity of bananas, a lack so profoundly moving to their elders. They do not do the stately waltz; they romp, they stomp. In all the surface manifestations of life they seem different. Beneath this veneer—thinner by far than those modern veneers that are so marvelous, they are youth growing out of the teens into the twenties—and facing the same old problems—with a new vocabulary.

Of the endless number of speeches a college president must make, those to students are of greatest importance—or can be. Certainly they constitute the most interesting audience he faces, if also the most difficult. This group is interesting because it is of high intelligence, and difficult for precisely the same reason. Students, particularly upperclassmen, can spot cant, pretense—sham in any form—with an almost unerring sense. They know, too, whether the talk is well prepared, well organized, or just some left-overs of "more important" messages now "thrown to the dogs."

They are usually extraordinarily polite. Many times, while presiding, I have sat in misery while a speaker who had no realistic idea as to what students like talked down to them, as though they were children. Even worse is the person who wants to employ "their own idiom" and gets his analogies to sport hideously snarled while urging them to "play the game." If there is one theme likely to rouse their fury it is coy references to the playing fields of Eton. Yet in the face of these intense provocations, when it was all I could do not to twitch the man's coat tails, the students sat like gentlemen, took it, and sent him away with enough applause to convince him (not a hard job!) that he had done well.

I have few illusions about their attitudes. There were instances when courtesy collapsed, when shuffled feet and rattled papers gave a speaker a very hard time. In no such episode, however regrettable, did he fail to deserve what he got. Often too their boredom was palpable, and while he ambled on vocally about their "bright, eager faces and shining eyes" they exhibited dead pans and glassy orbs.

On occasion they can show all the characteristics of a mob. One incident occurred while I was at Lawrence. The faculty had voted to restrict what had been a Thanksgiving week-end recess to a single holiday. A professor who was a perennial troublemaker there (and in his subsequent appointment in a university) suggested the students set up a claque. His cronies—a fraternity group—started it just as I stepped onto the platform. Whereupon the cry for a "vacation" was taken up and amounted to a din. I called on the president of the student body to restore at least momentary order, which he did with some difficulty. Then I presented a popular professor of piano who was apparently inspired by the excitement. I never heard her play so brilliantly. When she had gone only a few bars there was complete silence; at the end came a storm of applause—and no more was heard of a student "strike."

The only case of violence I recall occurred in a college where a classmate of mine was dean. The president was "exhausted" and went to Atlantic City—a long way from home—to relax. Unhappily for him he was observed several times relaxing with a blonde. When he returned to his campus, "rested and refreshed," and went to chapel to talk upon that part of his experience he thought would be uplifting to students, he was pelted with hymn books until literally driven from the building—and from office. That was detection of a fraud with a vengeance.

The students' reaction is swift. If a speaker gets off to a bad start it is rare indeed that he can recapture their lost interest. On the other hand, if he gains their attention by some clever gambit and then fails to deliver, their minds quickly wander and no new trick will lure them back toward his oratorical hook.

But let a speaker give them the respect they deserve, prepare well, say something, then stop, and they will treat him with a generosity that is overwhelming. If he does not repeat his jokes, assumes they can absorb solid material, and salts it moderately, that is the stuff to feed the troops.

There is more nonsense uttered about "compulsory

chapel" than almost any college topic. The difficulty has a twofold origin. First—and worst—not enough effort is put on the chapel program to make it interesting. It is a routine from which all zest and freshness have disappeared. I recall with vividness one instance from my undergraduate days. A professor noted for his muted mumbling and absence of articulation was in charge. He spoke as follows: "I am going to read from the one hundred and first psalm; that is, I will if I can get light enough to do so."

That shabby performance was only a somewhat extreme example of the general faculty attitude. I cannot remember that the president, or anyone else, said anything worth listening to during my four years. Platitudinous "challenges" to "prepare for life," vapid suggestions that we should "aim for leadership" came straight out of dusty files. They bored us. No wonder the students had no respect for the service. As with furniture, the library, or anything else about the college, their response reflects the real value—not in terms of mere verbal currency—put upon the matter by the president and the faculty.

The second difficulty with college chapel has been a stupid confusion about what is "compulsory" and what is not. Though the curriculum has many requirements, they are never called "compulsory." Every student at Brown, whether he liked it or not, had to learn to swim before he could be graduated. There was plenty of dislike of the requirement among those who did not enjoy water, but no protest at "compulsory" swimming. The central fact is that students are not assigned to colleges; they choose them for reasons as various as could possibly be imagined. When they select a college which has published its requirements, they elect to do what it prescribes for the attainment of a degree —and, perchance, an education. That includes chapel if attendance is an announced feature of its life.

I know of an admirable Catholic college. It does not bar

Jews or Protestants from admission, but if they decide to enroll they know they will go to Mass—and they do. No one apologizes for the requirement; and no one has a right to complain of "compulsory religion." The students were under no pressure to register; when they freely chose to do so they consented to abide by the regulations. I attended its commencement. Protestants and Jews knelt before the bishop to receive their diplomas; the only difference was that they did not kiss his ring.

When I contrast this forthright definition of what the college expects with the mealy-mouthed, apologetic evasions of so many colleges, it seems to me the lesson is clear. In one instance the institution stands for something, clearly, explicitly, and proudly. In most other cases the college is going forward with an inherited rite from which all substance has fled, and all the meaningless chatter about "compulsory religion" is a reflection of confusion and feebleness of purpose. There are over eighteen hundred institutions of higher education among which a student has a wide variety of choices; he is under no compulsion to enroll at one that has a requirement he dislikes.

Without some form of required assembly the president has lost a normal and regular forum for talks to students. If he has nothing worth saying, it is just as well; if, on the other hand, he can make a contribution to their educational outlook, it is a tragic loss.

VI

The Alumni

WHILE I was serving as the president's assistant for fund raising at Wesleyan, there was a vacancy in the office of alumni secretary, and for a time I ran that office also. When a regular appointee took over he was an intimate friend and we cooperated closely. During those months I found it was safe, as a working principle, to assume that the image of the college in the mind of an alumnus was to some extent a reflection of his undergraduate experience. It was not necessarily an exact and sharp reflection; time had dimmed the mirror somewhat; details were subordinated but the salient characteristics stood out.

For example, an alumnus whose undergraduate life had been dominated by his enthusiasm for rowing (this is a real case) could be interested in the institution as a whole only with the greatest difficulty because there was no longer a crew. The ancient shells which graced the high beams in the gymnasium were a constant reminder to him that "the place has gone backward" since his day.

This illustrates how "athletic alumni" get that way. Some sport had engaged their major energies, so memory and loyalty to that activity determine their measuring rod for the stature of the college. Similarly the alumnus whose main interest had been social—the Cotillion Club or the German

Club—is primarily concerned with that phase of life at a later time. Some undergraduates become saturated with fraternity; as the years go on fraternal loyalty far exceeds their attachment to the college.

The conclusion I reached then has been not only validated but reinforced through the years: the cultivation of the alumnus should start with his admission to the freshman class at the latest. With occasional exceptions that is a critical time. It is necessary at that moment to stress that college is primarily an intellectual experience. "Training" is involved; vocation is not negligible; social participation should be lively and interesting; physical activity should be vigorous. Nevertheless, the central objective is the cultivation of the life of the mind.

College years are not the most impressionable; that fact I might have learned elsewhere; actually I learned it from my brother. When I began as an instructor in college he was already teaching in high school. I could not understand how he could tolerate the brats; to me they seemed infuriating when I coached them in debate. For his part he could not understand why I chose to deal with young people after the plastic age had waned; to him the most impressionable years —and therefore the most exciting and rewarding to teach— were those of high school.

The obvious truth of my brother's conclusion suggested a revision of my timing so far as the education of the alumnus was concerned. It should start even before the prospective freshman applies for admission in the kind of publicity the colleges send out to preparatory students. I have studied college and university publications for sub-freshmen—as a matter of professional necessity—for thirty years. The astounding fact is their relatively slight emphasis on the intellectual life. This is one of the conspicuous evidences of that characteristic underestimation of students to which I have more than once referred.

One particular piece of promotional "literature" is vivid in my memory. It was prepared and dispatched by a great university whose president was almost fanatically dedicated to the liberal arts; he talked about the cultivation of the intellect virtually to the exclusion of everything else. Did the beautiful brochure of his university set forth these ideals and the opportunities for their fulfillment? Not at all. The cover photo showed a line of girls at archery; they were pretty girls, beautifully dressed in pleated shorts, and the camera angle might well have been determined by a Hollywood expert in cheesecake. Behind this beguiling cover were pages on social life, dormitory life, fraternities and sororities—and an occasional reference to courses of study.

The dean of students was a close friend of mine, so I asked how this sort of thing squared with the evangelistic fervor of the president for other values. He was familiar—as is every such officer—with the old saw, mentioned earlier, that the dean exists to make the college the kind of place the president insists it already is. But he gave it a reverse twist. With a broad grin he remarked that he and the other officers were happy to have the president preach his gospel away from the campus (which he usually was) so long as he left them free to manage the institution as they thought best.

That piece of merry cynicism might well be the end of the story, but it is not. Within the next four years a considerable number of colleges suddenly discovered the photogenic values of archery, a sport which had only a feeble existence, or none, theretofore. One college pamphlet after another, designed for sub-freshmen, blossomed out with an imitation of the original; they showed the same neglect of any intellectual emphasis.

In defense of such nonsense it was argued that "you must appeal to them at their own level; otherwise they will not be interested." Proponents could give figures as to the "success" of such literature in attracting enrollees. If one asked whether it also brought "students," the response was likely to be: "It's up to the faculty to make them students." This split between the responsibilities of the promotional staff (politely designated "admissions office") and the teaching faculty seemed to be the rule rather than the exception. The approach of the two groups tended to be antithetical rather than uniform. One of the very hardest tasks of a president is to induce those who prepare the bait for applicants to "sell what is on the shelves," not the country club features which are a part—and if in due proportion a legitimate part—of college. It would be stupid not to speak of sports and social life, but it is even more so not to lay adequate stress upon the central function of the institution.

The alumnus of tomorrow is already forming his image of the college when he makes his choice. If the promotional literature stresses high standards and the need for industry and discipline of the will to meet those requirements, admittedly a good many young people whose interests are primarily social or athletic will be repelled. That is all to the good. Just so many nascent "pestiferous alumni" will be eliminated at the least painful time. It is incontestable that some students who come to a college for the wrong reason catch a new vision while there and turn out successfully, but the number relative to the whole is distressingly small.

To return once more to my brother's observation: in seeking to influence the plastic age (pre-college, remember) it is important to direct the appeal primarily to that segment already predisposed to make the most of what the college has chiefly to offer. Education—and preparation for alumni status—offers problems enough under the most favorable circumstances. Those to whom the development of the higher mental processes offers no challenge will not be "lost"; they will not be deprived of any birthright to a degree. Other institutions can safely be trusted to bid them welcome to the happy bands of archers, swimmers, athletes, and socialites who inhabit their campuses.

If there is any validity whatever in the adage that begins "as the twig is bent," the alumnus justifies it. This fact partially accounts for the relatively slight influence most presidents exert over alumni opinion. The tenure of office of the majority of institutional heads is far too short for effective impact. The student spends over four years from the decision to apply for admission to attainment of his diploma. Thereafter the alumnus seldom exercises any notable influence until he has been out ten years; usually twenty is nearer the mark. Presidents who stay in office twenty-five years and reap the full fruits of their early cultivation of alumni are conspicuous by their rarity.

If this much is conceded, the question arises: "What shall the president do, seeing that his influence upon the dominant alumni group is likely to be marginal for a considerable period of time?" He had best not scatter his energies, but concentrate his fire as heavily as possible on one area—that which he regards as strategically the most important. The critical zone is educational policy and standards. He must seek to inure the alumni to the inevitability of change, and plead with them to accept it not only gracefully, as in defeat, but gladly, with pride.

There is no use to pretend that the task is easy. Undergraduates respond very quickly to alterations in program. They are not inhibited by nostalgia for days that are gone. They may have respect for the history of the institution, but they have no personal stake in it. The present fills their minds; and if they are persuaded that standards are advancing they will growl, of course, but beneath the surface there is a sense of achievement that braces their morale. Alumni, on the other hand, have not only pride in the past; in a very real sense they have possession of the past; it is their property. The college, as they knew it in student days, is the *real* college to most of them. This newer generation have entered upon a heritage which they do not seem to understand or appreciate. How can they? Are they not newcomers with no adequate sense of tradition? And this "new" president—does he not seek to lay profane hands upon sacred traditions?

While I was President Shanklin's assistant I heard this often enough about him. He had come from that terra incognita beyond the horizon—the Middle West. He did not "know New England," and so on. Because I was an alumnus, and had maintained close touch with the college even when in graduate school, I was exempt from alumni sniping on that score. But when I went to Lawrence I got the full treatment. Dr. Plantz was one of those rarities who had been president beyond the limits of memory of most active alumni. I was not only new, I was from that other "never-never land"—the East! I was not an alumnus, and in the words Meredith Willson's *Music Man* has made famous, "didn't know the territory." Moreover, I was in a hurry; there were so many things to be done, and the quicker the better.

The difficulty of convincing the graduates that change was unavoidable, and getting them to believe in the proposed alterations of policy, would have been infinitely more difficult if the alumni had been well organized. While, as I have said elsewhere, the alumni secretary declined to recognize my authority, he had no effective organizational structure to interpose as a barrier to any new program. When he was relieved of office, his successor was my own appointee, an alumnus, young, ambitious—and effective. He could get the ear of the skeptical and persuade; he could be a buffer for me as I had been earlier for another "stranger."

Not only was the alumni organization weak, the alumni magazine had only a limited circulation. Thus many alumni were totally uninformed. By a change in policy which sent it free to all alumni the new program was carried beyond the active few and the local group. Explanations went also to those afar off, many of whom had been wholly out of touch; they began to take an interest and to be heard.

Ultimately, too, mere iteration had an erosive effect upon opposition and a penetrative consequence with those who had been neutral or uninterested. One of the trustees, a true friend, once remarked in complete sincerity: "All your speeches are about the same subject; yet almost no one seems to realize it." He had exposed my secret; within the family I confessed my harp had only a single string. The variant effects came from changes in rhythm, in softness or loudness. But everywhere and always speeches were pleas for excellence in standards, for good teaching, for putting the intellectual life first.

During that era there was a good deal of agitation about the way in which alumni stopped reading upon graduation from college. I suspected that where it could be proved that they did not read as graduates, it was equally true that they had never been encouraged or required to read any great amount, or works of real significance, in college. With the aid of a grant from one of the foundations we set out to determine—in some rough way at least—what the facts were. We offered to send certain books to the alumni. At first my wife and I selected titles, read them all, and reviewed them; later we enlisted others to help in preparing the reviews. The experiment showed that, so far as Lawrence was concerned, the assertion that alumni stopped reading when their diplomas were won was radically incorrect. The demand for books was strong; that point having been made, the alumni were referred back to their local libraries. But there was a residue of value beyond mere demonstration; the alumni had been brought into direct intellectual contact with the college. Whenever that happens, their hospitality to program revisions is greatly increased.

A second experiment strengthened the impressions produced by the first. We set up, for a two- or three-day period, an "alumni college." It consisted of lectures and discussions under the leadership of the faculty. The purpose was not "instruction," much less "credit." The aim was to acquaint alumni with the current faculty members, to give them a first-hand contact and so help them believe that the later members of the teaching staff were "up to standard." The device is now widely followed in many institutions. Its effect was greatly to facilitate alumni acceptance of change, and reduce the frictions that retard new programs.

The move to Brown forced me to begin alumni cultivation all over again. I was the first non-Baptist in 173 years, and the first non-alumnus in nearly a century. In an Ivy university, where history is long and tradition a brooding presence, that was a considerable jolt to absorb. Moreover, there was a sound, if not over lively, alumni organization that could facilitate or obstruct the process of change.

There were assets of great weight on my side. Two of the most prominent alumni, Charles Evans Hughes, then Chief Justice, and John D. Rockefeller, Jr., came to my first commencement. The former spoke—eloquently—in behalf of my program, the latter served as chief marshal. It was impressive support from men whose credentials to represent the alumni were beyond challenge. Almost all the members of the Board of Fellows and the Board of Trustees were Brown graduates; many had been, others still were, active in the alumni organization. They had chosen me and, so long as they voted for my recommendations, shared responsibility.

It was not difficult, therefore, to find occasion to discuss policy at meetings of the alumni clubs across the country. However, a more continuous contact seemed desirable, and the best organ for that purpose was the alumni magazine. It was exceedingly well run by skillful and devoted men. Year after year they gave time and thoughtful care to its form and contents. Nevertheless, only about one-sixth of the alumni subscribed. This seemed to me to impair its effectiveness severely—the appeal failed to reach those who most needed it.

With what I hoped was gentle tact I proposed it be sent free to all alumni. The resistance was polite, but exceeding strong; my persistence was at least as firm. The crisis came at an annual meeting of the Alumni Council. One of my best friends among the trustees, who had done notable service as head of the audit committee, opposed the change. His argument was *ad hominem;* he asserted that, knowing me, it was inevitable that I would dominate the magazine; it would not be possible for one with my disposition to do otherwise. While he warmly supported my policies, he did not want criticism hushed or opposition deprived of a free forum.

I carried my point, though not without casualties. After fifteen years the value of reaching all alumni regularly has become fully apparent and has been generally accepted. The nature of the debate, however, inhibited me from exercising even a small measure of direct influence. Because of my friend's argument I felt I could never attend meetings of the board, lest I validate his assertion. I had to lean over backwards; if ever I made even so much as a suggestion, it was in the most indirect manner and with no hint of pressure behind it. Finally, the trustee who had prophesied I could not fail to dominate the publication chided me for not giving the magazine more guidance.

Actually intervention on my part was not necessary. Most of my administrative associates were Brown men; they were loyal collaborators in action, and persuasive exponents. The magazine continued to be edited by one of the group who had managed it before. He was—and is—a first-class editor, quick in his sympathies, generous in his judgments, devoted to the University. Under such circumstances the monthly was extraordinarily effective in support of essential change.

Nonetheless, as a matter of principle, I think an alumni magazine should always have a president's column. The office of the chief administrative officer is remote enough—indeed it is too remote—so that some human side of the president should find regular expression to all the alumni. He may not be a great leader, but he is a common symbol, and should have as much contact as possible with the whole constituency. Despite almost continuous travel his relationships with the individual alumnus are slight. He should have a regular means of speaking to them all through the magazine.

In talks to alumni clubs I followed the same pattern at Brown as at Lawrence—harping upon a continuous theme. While I spoke of football and sports often enough to show I was not hostile, others could and did expound athletic policy better than I. My energies went into a drum-fire of discussion of education and its progress in the University. As time went on those who asked me to speak knew what to expect; when they still urged me to come their blood was upon their own heads.

It is difficult to make clear how hard a president has to work to gain a real hearing—not just a formal acceptance of his presence. In the course of the years I have spoken as a guest to the alumni of many universities and colleges. One instance stands out in my mind as an illustration of this point.

The "new" president—in his fifth or sixth year—followed one long in office who was immensely popular with the alumni. Inevitably the successor was setting his own course of action, which built upon that of his predecessor, but also made some striking changes—among others a tremendous emphasis upon the intellectual life. I spoke first, and was treated with all the courtesy gentlemen show to guests. As a consequence it seemed to me not only a friendly but a relaxed audience and I looked forward with real anticipation to the president's speech.

No sooner was he on his feet than the hostility was so pronounced as to be palpable. His introduction had been not only brief, but cold. The applause that greeted him as he rose was so sparse as to be painful. During the next forty minutes my respect for him advanced by leaps and bounds. He made no concessions to prejudice at all; in clear and explicit terms he set forth his goals and the means he proposed in order to attain them. Never have I seen a man work harder. Perspiration dripped steadily from his chin to his necktie, until it was ruined beyond salvage. It was an example of courage even his enemies could not help but admire. The end of the story is inevitable: he stayed in office, stuck to his program, and increasingly won the bulk of the alumni to his support. Persistence put him in process of becoming a tradition himself.

One point a president must hammer home incessantly to the alumni—if the facts justify it. He must make the current faculty seem real and human to older graduates. As I have noted earlier, no phase of memory is so tinted with purple haze as the vision of "our" teachers. Even those whom the alumni as undergraduates looked upon with dislike are somehow reborn, in after years, with a quite different image. One professor of my acquaintance never recognized a student, even though he had seen him again and again. As a teacher he was known to be careless; his scholarship was in the past, if ever it had been alive; his own reading was trivial and escapist. Among undergraduates he was held in slight regard. Yet as alumni they adored him; he became a "tradition," and none of his successors could approach him in their affection.

This sort of synthetic reputation in retrospect is not at all uncommon. And, of course, there are memories of beloved teachers much more accurate and rational in their judgment. Both sorts of memory, however, make it hard for alumni to believe that the "new men" have the same dedication, like charm, equal skill, and true warmth. A president whose term of office spans any space of years finds it essential to make it patent that the modern faculty contains men of devotion, scholarship, teaching capacity, and attractive personalities. It is a theme which it is hard to overplay—for it is the key to confidence in the institution on the part of its most essential constituency.

In one aspect of relationship with the alumni I was a heretic at the beginning, in the middle, and at the end of my terms of office—and remain heretical in retirement. The atypical attitude relates to alumni funds—the annual contribution now a fixed feature of college and university promotion. My period of active concern with alumni giving covers the whole era of its significant development. When I went to work at fund raising there were a few institutions that made an appeal to the alumni for annual contributions, but the number was small and in all but a handful of instances the amounts were almost negligible, relative to total income and expenditure.

Early in that experience I observed that when there were economic troubles—"panic," "depression," "recession" (the styles in names change)—the colleges with large alumni funds were hardest hit. The reasons were not far to seek. Slowdowns in the economy tended to reduce dividends; an unusual number of mortgages and bonds went into default; thus the endowment income was curtailed, sometimes sharply. The student body also shrank; many who had planned on going to college could not; therefore tuition income declined. In an effort not to lose too many students, scholarship grants and loans were stepped up; so income from students was further decreased. To top it all alumni giving sagged noticeably in many cases and alarmingly in some.

Of all sources of income the annual alumni fund proved the most volatile. When income from endowment reflected boom times and student fees shot up, so did alumni giving. It encouraged budget expenditures—on assumptions of stable income—which had to be cut drastically when not one but all sources of income fell—alumni giving most of all.

In some cases that came under my observation the consequences were no less than tragic. In one conspicuous instance the junior faculty was virtually liquidated. This was not only hard on them, as individuals; it was disastrous to the essential age balance of the faculty; the average age of teachers in service shot up sharply. The energy, enthusiasm, and freshness of younger teachers were lost. Worst of all there was no body of young men and women being tested in the local situation to see whether they merited promotion and the grant of tenure.

The adverse effect on the teaching and scholarly output was striking. The damage was not limited to the period of the depression; it was noticeable for several years thereafter. Stability is essential to progress; there must be change, but it should be orderly and controlled. Drastic interruption of the normal processes is bad for an institution.

For these reasons I have always advocated having the alumni fund assigned to capital expenditures. When that is done one of the least stable income items is eliminated from the budget. The president is not encouraged upon adventures which may suddenly have to be dropped. Using alumni gifts for capital is also good promotion; there is an opportunity to set challenging goals before the graduates. Some necessary building is projected; it becomes a center of interest. Money is accumulated for a year or two during the planning stage; it continues to come in during construction. Funds can be borrowed to complete the building because alumni giving will soon liquidate the debt. By then there is some new, dramatic project.

The growth of higher education has been steady; therefore the need for new construction is continuous. But a study of what customarily happens shows that common practice does not keep pace with the need. Usually there are surges of activity—such as followed the Harkness gifts, for example—and then long periods when obsolescence becomes marked. In some great institutions periods as long as twenty years have passed with no significant improvement of plant and facilities. Then comes a "drive," a disruption of normal promotion to abnormal proportions, a flurry of construction, followed by another sterile era.

There are a few institutions which have followed the program I have urged, and they have done it with conspicuous success. Twice I succeeded in having the Brown Corporation adopt the principle as a statement of policy. It was one of those instances when a president's recommendation is accepted without adequately deep conviction. As a consequence, the next time there was alarm about the size of the "deficit," the alumni fund was appropriated for current use instead of being devoted to capital purposes. My successor seems to have succeeded in reestablishing the better policy—how permanently time alone will tell.

During the forty years I have been concerned with administration, the place of alumni in the management and support of universities and colleges, and in recruiting students for them, has undergone a startling change. From mere sentimental attachment they have gone forward to large shares of responsibility. Almost all alumni bodies are now represented on governing boards; their magazine has the force of public opinion in influencing policy within the institution; their gifts have become major sources of enlarged service.

Occasionally this rise to power has produced acute friction. In one institution where I had a lively, but detached, interest, the president had never been popular with the alumni. So far as I could see, he made no effort to win them over, but went his own serene way for many years, apparently untroubled by their hostility. Suddenly the alumni organization decided that alumni gifts, raised through its efforts, should be spent in accordance with its own desires. The sum, while not large by current standards, was very considerable. Quite apart from the question of principle involved, its loss to the budget in which it had long been firmly embedded would have been severe.

This declaration of independence upon the part of the alumni organization went far beyond harassment of the president, which perhaps it was intended to be. It was a challenge to the authority and responsibility of the governing board. The trustees reacted with unaccustomed and unexpected vigor, not so much in support of the president as in defense of their own charter responsibilities. The row was unedifying, damage to all concerned was considerable, but, inevitably, the authorized governing board won both the battle and the war. After some changes in the leading personalities involved in the fracas, matters went smoothly for many years thereafter.

The phrase "pestiferous alumni" was coined, I believe,

by a young faculty man who never had to work with them. It would be folly to deny that some are pestiferous; they have hobby horses—athletics, religion, morals, liquor—that they ride incessantly, at inappropriate moments and improper places. But, relative to the total, such people are few, though on tense occasions I found it hard to believe. The last thirty years have seen a development of responsible alumni interest and support that is no less than amazing. The president who does not know that and shape his course to take advantage of it is not up to his job.

VII

The Public

THE last element in the constituency of a college with which the president has to deal is the public. If he believed a small fraction of the warnings given him as he undertakes the office he would be terrified. He will be told of the quixotism of public favor, how some small incident can turn public opinion into an adverse channel. "Public relations," he will be informed, is vital to the support and progress of the institution, and must take precedence over other factors at all times.

Such assertions are nonsense. The best public relations program is to do a job in a conscientious and workmanlike manner, with mind and heart intent upon the educational program and its fulfillment—and no concern for the grandstand. I have seen many administrations wrecked through attempts to pander to what was assumed to be "public opinion." Many of the worst practices in recruiting and subsidizing athletes have grown out of an effort to please "downtown" with a winning team. When all the hoop-la has died away, it is discovered too late that "downtown" in that context does not consist of the solid citizens but of people who can do the college no good—and have no interest in doing so, even if they could.

A great deal of money has been lost by thinking it is

essential to buy locally because the local merchants are important to the support of the institution. Soon after the new business manager was installed at Lawrence he was offered a "cut" if he bought goods at list price and did not insist upon wholesale rates for large orders. He discovered that dormitory matrons were buying cereals and canned goods in family sizes—at retail. When he declined the graft and said that supplies of many kinds would be bought from the lowest bidder, the worriers among trustees asked, "Is it wise? It is annoying 'downtown.' "

The reverse was the truth. As soon as merchants realized that the affairs of the college were going to be handled in a businesslike manner they responded with a new respect—and better bids. More and more business was done locally because the merchants knew that college credit was flawless and bills would be paid so promptly as to warrant cash discounts. The relationship was increasingly one of mutual regard. To have sought to "buy" respect by unbusinesslike procedures would have been self-defeating.

In somewhat the same way I was urged, again and again, not to become "controversial" by taking public positions with which there would be disagreement in "influential quarters." It was not advice that appealed to either my temperament or my judgment. I have known too many college presidents so careful not to offend that though they talked more and more they said less and less. When that process went far enough, they were neglected, or viewed with contempt. A president is a public figure. He should make clear that his views are not necessarily those of his faculty colleagues or the trustees. Once he has made those points explicit he should speak his mind, if he has one. It should be done on most matters with persuasive good temper; but there are occasions when indignation and even wrath are not only appropriate but necessary.

One of these espisodes occurred while I was at Lawrence.

The students, like others across the nation, wanted to demonstrate on behalf of peace. It is hard, now, to recapture the mood of a quarter of a century ago. Peace had become a fighting word. There is no question that some of the propaganda was Red-inspired, that some of the organizations were Communist fronts, others deeply infiltrated. However, the students at Lawrence exhibited none of those symptoms. They went about their plans soberly and with my approval. I was out of sympathy with "peace strikes"; they seemed to me the wrong approach. The students agreed their demonstration would be no "strike."

They proposed a parade on behalf of peace. Surely that is one of the fundamental aspirations of mankind; the word has an almost hypnotic attraction today. It was—and is—a basic policy of the United States. This nation was the instigator and signatory of the Pact of Paris—the Kellogg-Briand pact, which became, by ratification, part of the law of the land. The plans for the demonstration were in support of that policy.

Though not required by city ordinance to do so, the students asked the city officials for a permit to parade, which was granted. Indeed the chief of police hired a horse to lead the procession. Suddenly, on someone's inspiration, he reversed himself. When the procession formed, the campus was ringed with police with side arms and clubs in hand. The parading students remained on the campus; they did carry signs. One which seemed to give offense called them "Veterans of Future Wars"; a more precise definition of their status would be difficult to devise in the light of the Second World War. They made satiric references to the bonus, then at issue, but none so pointed or severe as those of Presidents Roosevelt, Hoover, Coolidge, and Harding.

A small group of students left the campus to go to a

nearby restaurant. The search for food is a continuous performance with young people. Police set upon them and beat them up; the chief admitted they were not parading, they had committed no breach of the peace, they had done nothing provocative. No student was arrested; no charges were preferred.

It might seem that the defense of students in their orderly exercise of the right of peaceful assembly and of individuals to use public streets without molestation would be easy. Ah! but it was not good public relations! There ensued the customary tempest in a teapot. My stubborn support of the students' rights would be taken as advocation of their supposed "cause," the peace demonstration. No matter what I said to the contrary, I was defending "radicals," "pacifists" —and so on.

This is the ordinary, every day sort of thing with which a president must live. After some unexpected football victory students will want a bonfire and fail to discriminate adequately between burnable waste and private property. They will be noisy—even late at night! The list of occasions when students irritate their elders is as long as the pen holds ink. Every episode, however trivial, will bring letters to the newspapers deploring modern youth, castigating pusillanimous administrators who do not control them.

The plain, unvarnished fact is that students are more orderly, more law-abiding, more tractable than in those earlier times which people who scorn history so glorify. One has only to know something of drunkenness in the eighteenth century to see how far we have come. A grave and reverend Fellow at Brown told me as I recounted complaints of student ebullience that half his class were sleeping drunk on the College Green following some celebration sixty years before. Another, for several years the senior Fellow, told me how he had broken the plaster in his room and pried the lath from the studs to burn in his fireplace. Yet people howl over modern "destruction of property."

Considering the number of students enrolled in the colleges and universities of the nation, their record of peace and good order is remarkable. Discipline is no longer so brutal as once it was, but it is not so quixotic either. It is swifter, more discriminating, more effective. Even more important, student self-government is vastly better than in the "good old days" that never were.

A sense of humor, quiet discipline of students who go too far, and silence before one's critics seem to be the best prescription for a college president. There is no hope of persuading elders who have lost faith in the younger generation that they are wrong. There is equally no sense in trying to gag or hobble young people.

The main theme to expound to the public is the educational objective, and the means for attaining it. In season and out of season, year after year, hammer away at that theme. The initial response will be disheartening; the ultimate result will never be wholly satisfying. But there will be progress. As the business community will respect fiscal integrity, so the larger community will appreciate, at least in some degree, high scholastic standards.

When a scion of some "prominent family" is denied admission because of a poor preparatory record and low aptitude tests, the first reaction will be shock and incredulity. The secondary effect is to increase respect and confidence in educational integrity.

Even in publicity it is well to harp on educational matters. This is rugged doctrine. Most newspapers have a sizable staff of sports reporters; if they have a full-time man covering education it is a miracle. Their readiness to print the picture of a May Queen is to their eagerness to photograph a Phi Beta Kappa as quicksilver to lead. So be it. Let them print the one they like, but never fail to send a well-done release about the other. The results of persistence—and skill—are astonishing. Although they may not hunt out the latter type of story, they will print it on the theory that names make news.

It is certainly true that public support is essential; it is certainly not true that public relations should take precedence over all considerations at all times. Public support will not come, significantly or as a rule, from success in athletics. It will not develop on a significant scale through publicity dodges and public relations tricks. It is not true that every mention of the name of the college is "all to the good" or that "every knock is a boost." Soundness of program and integrity are the associations in the public mind that bring the necessary measure of support.

L'Envoi

THIS book was not designed as a definitive study of a characteristic and unique American institution—the college presidency. Its purpose is far less pretentious; it is merely a personal account of how one man in his youth became involved, and what impressions various aspects of official activity left upon his mind at the end of his tenure of office. It makes no pretense to supply a guide. There are as many ways to meet the tasks as there are individuals who with their whole minds and hearts set out to undertake them. There is no mold in which college presidents can be shaped—and called good. Each must do what he does in his own way.

It is an arduous life. Those who told me that my nervous system was not attuned to its tensions, nor my constitution fitted for its rigors, were almost right. Again and again at the end of the academic year, I was spent, physically and spiritually. Hang on, get through commencement, then relax enough to recover energy and faith; that was the prescription. For thirty years it worked, sometimes by a narrow margin, at others by a wide one.

The best definition of what the life is like appears in another context entirely. In *Swann's Way*, Marcel Proust writes: "There are mountainous, uncomfortable days, up which one takes an infinite time to pass, and days downward sloping, through which one can go at full tilt, singing as one goes."

People who knew of the enormous strains that go with the job have asked, many times, "Would you do it again?" Of course I would; I could do no other. The opportunities so far outweigh the heartbreaks that to evade the responsibility would be folly.

Finally, one of the amusements of retirement is reflection upon the processes of history-making. Life is one thing; history is quite another. The historian tries to recreate, from "objective" data, an image of the past—some man, some event, some era. Usually this takes a long while—it is said that only time can supply perspective. But the process begins at once, and if one disappears from the scene it is speeded up. It consists in making very large generalizations from random particulars; by neglecting detail, as it must, it produces a portrait—or a caricature—that "captures the essence" of the individual. That "essence" is almost—if not quite—as much a reflection of the values of the estimator as of the estimated.

I have now been out of office long enough—and at Lawrence and Brown so infrequently—that I can observe this process taking place. This volume is no effort to create an image; life is too complex and experiences too various for any individual to succeed if he were to try, and I have no temptation to make the attempt. Let these chapters be read—if at all—as a personal view of an institution—not an institutional view of a person.